David L. Laing

Minds Beyond Time:
A Cosmic Colloquium

*A fanciful colloquy among some of
history's most notable minds*

Cosmic Art Center

Published in the United States of America

Cosmic Art Center
62 Cedar St.
Apt. 601
Seattle, Washington 98121

Paperback ISBN **978-1-960089-06-9**

Dedicated to all those who dream beyond Time and any distinctions between past, present and future.

Contents

Foreword

From the imagination of visionary (and somewhat eccentric) writer and artist David L. Laing comes **Minds Beyond Time: A Cosmic Colloquium**, a fanciful colloquy among some of history's most notable minds.

What would happen if history's greatest thinkers, philosophers, scientists, artists, musicians, writers, religious figures, political leaders, tyrants, and villains, along with a few deities, archetypes, and mythological beings for good measure, came together, beyond the confines of time and space, for just one day? Author Laing's answer is **Minds Beyond Time**, an illuminating, entertaining and delightfully bizarre thought experiment from the depths of his wild imagination.

Imagine a school run by Professor Plato, where students like Freud, Mozart, Socrates, King Solomon, Da Vinci, Jesus, Buddha, and Shakespeare engage in a spirited classroom debate, while Ocar Wilde quips, Isadora Duncan dances down the aisles, and Bach serves coffee. In the courtyard, the "troubled kids" like Hitler, Stalin, Nero, Trotsky and Genghis Khan gang up with Satan to argue world domination strategies while Dali smokes a peace pipe with Black Elk and Hannibal rides an elephant. Imagine a school where the popular girls are Joan of Arc, Cleopatra, Nefertiti, Catherine the Great, and Mother Mary, and the class clown is the literal embodiment of "The Fool" archetype.

This is a small glimpse into a day in the life at Plato's Academy. Written in the form of a *Platonic Dialog* between these notable figures and many, many others, the magical realism in **Minds Beyond Time** allows each character to embody their most essential nature, and engage with other luminaries from different eras and corners of the world that would be otherwise impossible. The dialog and interactions that unfold give insight into each person's life, as they explore their thoughts and theories, share their histories and notable quotations, and demonstrate their quirks and eccentricities.

Unbound from the constraints of time and space, they explore the nature of reality, mind, art, society, religion and the great mysteries of life together. Some inspire each other and expand their minds by sharing ideas. Some argue bitterly and attempt to discredit each other. Some dance, sing, create and laugh together. Some tease and bully and plot each other's destruction. There's no limit to what can happen in Plato's Academy!

Laing invites the reader to suspend disbelief, embrace the impossible, and let your imagination and curiosity guide you through this one of a kind journey.

Minds Beyond Time

I

Professor Plato's Classroom
Ancient School of Dialog and Learning
Somewhere outside of space and time

PROFESSOR PLATO: *(Bespectacled and wearing a tweed jacket with no tie, he scans over the classroom.)* Who are we missing? Anyone seen Ludwig?

ERIK SATIE: Late as usual!

WOLFGANG AMADEUS MOZART: Like his Quartets...which, by the way I memorized all in one sitting.

Isadora Duncan enters, barefoot as usual, carrying her Grecian vase filled with flowers, which she carefully places on her desk.

PROFESSOR PLATO: *(Eyeing her bare feet, following her till she gets seated)* You look like you are in a daze, Isadora.

ISADORA DUNCAN: Wagner! No one ever got it right! *(Mary glances up with her maternal demeanor as Isadora looks straight at her.)* Dancing his music! By the way, where is Richard?

SIGMUND FREUD: Are you fixated on your feet?

ISADORA DUNCAN: Not consciously, "Siggy." It is me trying to contact that Unconscious realm of Mother Earth. It grounds my dance to allow my mind to reach for the clouds.

SIGMUND FREUD: You are fantasizing now?

Carl Jung, who had been meditating on a strange symbol in the corner of the classroom, suddenly speaks up.

CARL JUNG: She is her own Greek symbol in movement.

MARY: Blessed be those who whirl, spin and dance!

Hildegard von Bingem has arrived ever so discreetly.

HILDEGARD VON BINGEM: If I had only been around I would have backed you, Isadora. I get you!

Mozart sings notes now coming through his head.

WOLFGANG AMADEUS MOZART: Who has something to write on?

JOSEPH HAYDN: Here, "son." I thought you might suddenly need this parchment paper.

Isadora hears Mozart singing and starts to dance. Her white tunic gown gently whirls. In the background we hear a wheezing and coughing. It is young Beethoven over by where the coats are hung, already looking disheveled and straining to hear Mozart.

PROFESSOR PLATO: Aristophanes! *(Plato shouts out.)*

Aristophanes is looking out the window towards the birds in a tree in the schoolyard.

ARISTOPHANES: Free to be carefree. Look at the birds!

LUDWIG VON BEETHOVEN: *(Nodding in the direction of Mozart)* That is my dream teacher, one who has real steps to emulate. *(He wheezes more as he runs his hand through disheveled hair.)*

ISADORA DUNCAN: *(Whirls towards Beethoven)* Come and dance!

PROFESSOR PLATO: Artists! There is no room for them here. I am trying to create a New Republic!

ARISTOPHANES: Your ideal republic is for the birds!

Freud, Michelangelo and Leonardo da Vinci are off to the side talking together.

SIGMUND FREUD: Ahhhhh!…Sublime…sublimation. How can it be captured?

MICHAELANGELO: By chipping away at it. We are all in search of our own "David!"

Young King Solomon appears out of nowhere.

KING SOLOMON: For my father, nothing was set in stone.

LEONARD DAVINCI: *(Brushing back his beautiful locks of flaxen hair)* Whatever I can't paint I invent. I was born after being reborn.

Aristotle now makes his appearance at the doorway to the classroom.

ARISTOTLE: I think they called it the "Renaissance"…our baby.

Socrates follows Aristotle inside

SOCRATES: What is it...was it...or will be it?

HILDEGARD VON BINGEM: Some things are not to be questioned, but just taken on faith.

ALEXANDER THE GREAT: I conquer what I believe, rather than I believe what I can conquer—though both happen to be true.

Samuel Becket was one of the first to get there and was not about to go anywhere.

SAMUEL BECKET: What are we waiting for?

William Shakespeare has come in and found a desk right in the front of the classroom.

WILLIAM SHAKESPEARE: I didn't ever wait, though my poor "Hamlet" sure did.

PROFESSOR PLATO: I realize there appears to be no ideal form to our class, nevertheless there is—it just can't be seen.

SOCRATES: I question your "forms," though I've never seen them.

PROFESSOR PLATO: Do you also question music, having never seen any of its notes?

Plato falls silent as if listening to his own silence.

LUDWIG VON BEETHOVEN: I do not question music, although I can neither see nor hear it!

In one of the other corners of the classroom, young King Solomon is playing with some blocks, looking as if he were building a miniature size temple.

PROFESSOR PLATO: Solomon! What are you doing over there?

SOLOMON: Just wondering what it may look like...

PROFESSOR PLATO: ...look like?

SOLOMON: My temple!

PROFESSOR PLATO: *(Closes his eyes to access his Imagination...then opens them)* I can visualize it now!

WILLIAM SHAKESPEARE: A man with no imagination has no wings.

Albert Einstein appears through his own "spacetime continuum."

ALBERT EINSTEIN: Imagination is more important than knowledge!

He then looks around for his violin case, opens it, takes out the bow and starts to "bow the air," as if playing with invisible elemental spirits.

Johann Sebastian Bach, who has been out of the class returns and after not speaking for all that time blurts out:

JOHANN SEBASTIAN BACH: The two need to be harmonized: knowledge and imagination.

Bach looks over at Einstein and his bow and begins hearing his first violin partita playing in his head. The music magically becomes audible in the room.

Jesus has miraculously manifested himself in the classroom and has been silent up into this moment.

JESUS: Johann, you are my friend and my happiness.

JOHANN SEBASTIAN BACH: All my work is dedicated to you. I know that you loved to dance when imparting wisdom to your disciples.

JESUS: Everything I said you "noted!" Then your organ spread the word.

John Dowland pops in, to not get an "absent" for class.

JOHN DOWLAND: You took my lute and made it sound like a flute.

PROFESSOR PLATO: In our hospitals we have an entire ward dedicated to musical therapy.

JOHANN SEBASTIAN BACH: Makes perfect sense, though I never knew.

There is a pause as the classroom door rattles and opens. George Sand enters, smoking a cigar, and takes off her top hat. Beethoven glares at her, not recognizing her.

GEORGE SAND: I've got nowhere to hang my hat. *(She drops the hat on the floor.)* Guess I'll just leave it there.

PROFESSOR PLATO: Ms. Sand! Please! You know the rules.

GEORGE SAND: You mean those to be broken?

Beethoven starts coughing again because of all the cigar smoke. Sand makes her way over to the desk next to where Fredrick Chopin is sitting.

GEORGE SAND: Is this taken?

FREDERICK CHOPIN: *(Elegantly and shyly, stuttering)* DDDDDon't believe so.

George Sand tosses down a book on Chopin's desk.

GEORGE SAND: My latest potboiler!

George Sand, still standing, looks around defiantly at the rest of the class.

GEORGE SAND: I am not alone. I have many friends in high places.

More confusion at the door of the classroom as Joan of Arc tries to force her way in, leading her favorite horse.

PROFESSOR PLATO: Joan, get that beast out of here. The revolution is over!

JOAN OF ARC: It is just beginning. Your classes don't speak to the French. We want to change everything!

Sand picks up her book off Chopin's desk and holds it up.

GEORGE SAND: I'm done with writing trash like this. *(Pointing to Joan of Arc)* You will be the heroine of my new novel!

Beethoven is startled to discover there is a massive horse at his side and falls to the ground. Mozart rushes over to help.

WOLFGANG AMADEUS MOZART: You hurt?

LUDWIG VON BEETHOVEN: *(Yelling out)* I have been waiting for the right moment to ask you to tutor me. Haydn is too busy...especially with my new voices that won't stop singing in my head. It's an idea to add to the symphony!

With all this going on, Michelangelo stands in the center of the classroom staring fixedly at the ceiling.

PROFESSOR PLATO: Michelangelo! What is so interesting up there that you cannot focus on our classwork?

MICHELANGELO: What?! *(Coming back from his reverie to reality)* Everything! Everything is up there!

Seated by himself, as if he were alone on a mountaintop, is Lao-Tzu.

LAO-TZU: Which is what?

PROFESSOR PLATO: I did not know you were even here with us.

LAO-TZU: I am and am not. The only class worth having is the one that you create with your own path. Pure class!

George I. Gurdjieff was also one of the first to arrive and is off by himself with a bottle of Russian-made vodka on his desk and making imaginary digging movements with an imaginary shovel. As if awakening from his imaginary activity, he blurts out in a bellowing voice:

G.I. GURDJIEFF: We are all asleep here...*(Looks around slowly)* with the exception of maybe you.

Gurdjieff looks in the direction of Lao-Tzu.

PROFESSOR PLATO: Well, if it isn't our favorite "hole-digger!"… deciding If he can condescend to finally join us.

G.I. GURDJIEFF: What you so flippantly refer to as "hole-digging" has gotten many a lost soul back on track.

PROFESSOR PLATO: Hey, George! Who is running the show here anyway?

Gurdjieff nonchalantly reaches over to his bottle of vodka and takes a healthy swig.

PROFESSOR PLATO: *(Looking with disapproval at Gurdjieff)* Don't we have a ruling on this?

Gurdjieff continues disregarding the frown from Plato and guzzles.

ISADORA DUNCAN: I dig it George! As much as I do your Sacred Dances!

Gurdjieff looks surprised and stops his drink in midair to see who was talking. He examines her gown and Grecian vase and recognizes Isadora.

G.I. GURDJIEFF: I'm just surprised our paths never crossed before now. Without a doubt, your reputation precedes you.

JESUS: I did those dances together with my disciples. We both drank from that same well…that same one that your "diggers" have dug so well.

Aristotle has a quizzical look on his face as if just now awakening to another new thought.

ARISTOTLE: I may have been wrong regarding all of that subject categorization and knowledge division.

ISADORA DUNCAN: It's difficult to see the whole if you have not encircled it at least once in the Dance role.

G.I. GURDJIEFF: There is movement and there is MOVEMENT!

PROFESSOR PLATO: You were my protege and child prodigy, Aristotle. Don't sell yourself short here!

JOHANN SEBASTIAN BACH: Whoever can dance what I've composed has a chance to lead a life wonderfully transposed.

Bach leaves the room, following some mysterious inner guidance.

ISADORA DUNCAN: *(Shouting after him as he leaves)* You have to dance it to really "see" your music, Johann.

MARY: I always knew my son was a "mover" from the beginning.

She looks over at Jesus with Motherly love.

Bach re-enters carrying a small round platter of mugs with coffee.

PROFESSOR PLATO: Now what's going on?!

JOHANN SEBASTIAN BACH: Never too early or too late for coffee. How do you think I managed to write a new cantata for every Sunday?

Bach is now offering and serving coffee to everyone present, as the "Coffee Cantata" becomes audible in the background, emanating from an unknown source. During this time Alexander Pushkin has come around, that black Ethiopian ex-slave who became the symbol of Russian literature.

ALEXANDER PUSHKIN: Who knows where it first originated? *(The room is silent, as nobody seems to know the answer. Pushkin nods to Bach.)* From a small village in Ethiopia called Kaffa in my mother country.

A previously unseen hatch in the floor opens up. Fyodor Dostoyevsky emerges from an underground refuge, grasping a bundle of "notes."

FYODOR DOSTOYEVSKY: We know that you are an illegitimate heir to the throne of Russian literature.

Leo Tolstoy has also just made it there after an apparently epic journey through snow and revolution.

LEO TOLSTOY: It was the Prince who promoted you up from your position of a slave.

FYODOR DOSTOYEVSKY: That same one who finally reprieved me at the last second from the sure-death of a firing squad?

ALEXANDER PUSHKIN: Words are color-blind. It was that branch of my poetry that moved me up the Prince's family tree.

Plato now takes a generous sip of coffee.

PROFESSOR PLATO: Even though coffee has been served, class is still very much in session. We all know Dostoyevsky is no "idiot," nor is his Prince Myshkin from in his novel.

ALEXANDER PUSHKIN: Actually Fyodor, your "Notes From the Underground" inspired me to get to where I was ultimately bound.

LEO TOLSTOY: Fyodor was the first "modern" writer to recognize and use freely the subconscious in his work.

SIGMUND FREUD: Not before my discovery!

LUDWIG VON BEETHOVEN: Yes Dr. Freud! *(He bellows out)* I too have accessed those realms before you could identify them with words.

PROFESSOR PLATO: Ok ok, there is nothing to quibble about here. We are now all in the same "boat"...that I am working to keep afloat.

Arthur Rimbaud had staggered in just after the coffee service.

ARTHUR RIMBAUD: Yeah! I call it the "drunken boat."

George Sand takes another deep puff on her cigar.

GEORGE SAND: How would you really know, anyway? You were busy running arms to Algiers.

Thomas Edison now stands over by the light switch. He notices Michelangelo has gone back to staring at the ceiling.

THOMAS EDISON: My arms were never running but always working to finally come up with that!

Edison points dramatically towards the light bulb Michelangelo continues to stare at.

MICHELANGELO: Suddenly I can see it—all of Creation on the ceiling of a dome—the mind is now finally at home!

THOMAS EDISON: Whatever you are talking about, it appears a "light" just went on.

Grigori Rasputin has arrived in his monk's habit and looks suspiciously at everyone as he fingers his bushy beard. Plato appears to be unalarmed by his presence, as he apparently has seen it all at one time or another.

GRIGORI RASPUTIN: I not only can see the light but "feel" the electricity in my veins. *(He pauses and closes his eyes, going inside.)* I am the light!

William Blake is now present and obviously in an enraptured state.

WILLIAM BLAKE: I can clearly see it and almost touch it!

PROFESSOR PLATO: Bach! Please go get a cup of coffee for Mr. Blake. We need to reel him in. You, too, Rasputin. Get ahold of yourself. This is the very reason why I will have no artists, as well as no mystics, in my Ideal Republic!...Pure Troublemakers!

Johann Wolfgang von Goethe walks solemnly through the door, looking as sorrowful as Young Werther.

JOHANN WOLFGANG VON GOETHE: There is no solidity in your "ideal form." It is as ephemeral as any of Blake's visions which you so easily disregard.

Plato motions for Goethe to take a seat and tries to get some order in the class. Rebellious Niccolo Paganini stands up defiantly and mimicking the emotional playing of the violin. His music starts to be heard in the background. He is dressed all in black with wild hair. We see his elongated fingers moving as if reaching for far-flung notes.

NICCOLO PAGANINI: I need no viola to play the only show that I know.

Outraged at this musical outburst Chopin stands up, visibly agitated.

FREDERICK CHOPIN: Sit down devil. We are not impressed!

Franz Liszt barges into the classroom in the middle of Chopin's outburst. He is very elegantly dressed for a student, and carries what looks to be an orchestra leader's baton.

FRANZ LISZT: Let him go on my friend. You have had your day in the Mazurka sun.

George Sand walks to Chopin's side, balancing the still lit cigar in the air.

GEORGE SAND: Now we are finally having some real fun!

Oscar Wilde is also there, in a fur coat to keep warm.

OSCAR WILDE: Yes, fun it is. I, myself am so clever that sometimes I don't understand a single word of what I am saying.

PROFESSOR PLATO: That is exactly the kind of thing I want to guard against. Artists!!

Isadora Duncan holds up her Grecian urn again.

ISADORA DUNCAN: It is all designed here and up to me to express its uniqueness. From your own people, Professor. How can you be so against that?

She continues moving around in a circle still, of course, barefoot.

Darwin still remains seated. He imitates the movements of a fish desperately attempting to move out onto dry land.

CHARLES DARWIN: Is this really helping our evolution?

Thomas Jefferson, now seated near the front of the classroom, holds a quill and a scroll of paper.

THOMAS JEFFERSON: No, but it is helping our cause for independence.

NICCOLO PAGANINI: *(Still wildly gesticulating)* I can easily make one string sound as four.

Paganini's music reaches a crescendo as Hildegard Von Bingem breaks into raucous laughter.

HILDEGARD VON BINGEM: Never saw anything like this in the Abbey.

Hildegard starts singing improvised notes following along with the sound of the violin.

Suddenly the music stops as abruptly as it had begun. A woman who had been silent so long slowly rises to her feet. Nefertiti turns to her side for all to see her profile.

NEFERTITI: My head inspired a civilization!

LEONARD DAVINCI: Where have you been all my life? You are the African madonna!

Leonardo takes out his charcoal and starts to sketch her. Michelangelo is disgusted.

MICHELANGELO: She is much too thin to sculpt and way too dark to paint!

LEONARD DA VINCI: Don't worry about it. Your ceiling is already too crowded.

Mahatma Gandhi had been silent too, until now, but rises up from his desk to speak.

MAHATMA GANDHI: Hey, can't we just get along! *(He adjusts his robes and walks up to the front where Plato is teaching.)* I have nothing more to say. *(He slowly adjusts his robe and calmly walks back to his seat.)*

Gautama Buddha sits in blissful meditation.

GAUTAMA BUDDHA: He is telling us to continue our journey, to walk our own path.

MAHATMA GANDHI: The satisfaction is all in the effort.

FRIEDRICH NIETZSCHE: And our "will to power"!...which goes way beyond good and evil.

WILLIAM SHAKESPEARE: Nothing good or bad but thinking makes it so.

PROFESSOR PLATO: Your mind determines your find.

Plato is now more animated, realizing the job he has here at hand, and shows that in his body language.

NEFERTITI: *(Still in profile)* The head is the mushroom. Inside its "room" is the entire trip.

LEONARD DA VINCI: After my "Madonna and Child" painting you will be my first "Black Madonna."

Michelangelo is back to just staring at the ceiling waiting for his dome vision to expand.

FRIEDRICH NIETZSCHE: We are all still a slave to your cave, Professor Plato, mistaking those shadows on the wall projected by the fire, thinking that is all.

Dante Alighieri, after a long exile, now returns to Plato's class after having received an invitation like the rest of the students. He stands along the back wall in his usual long dignified robe, called a "lucco," with his hair concealed beneath the characteristic Florentine hood.

DANTE ALIGHIERI: I am reminded of my Divine Comedy and its first book, "Inferno." From a little spark may burst a flame with no particular name. The secret to getting things done is to act.

Sir Winston Churchill is also in the class, seated with coat and typical top hat and cane. He now lights up a cigar and smokes, mirroring George Sand. They eye each other through their rings of smoke.

WINSTON CHURCHILL: When you are going through Hell, keep going.

He tips his hat to Dante. Beethoven is seen still straining to hear everything using his ear-horn.

LUDWIG VON BEETHOVEN: (Yelling angrily) If it wasn't for my muse of music I would have ended it all. My music made my heaven out of hell.

FYODOR DOSTOYEVSKY: If I had known you at the time of writing I would have added you to the Karamazov family as the fifth brother.

Vaslav Nijinsky dances his way through the door dressed as his "faun." Isadora gives him an approving look of support.

VASLAV NIJINSKY: I am god!

JESUS: But it isn't possible that I am YOUR son!

SIGMUND FREUD: I just love these crises of identity. It is a pity we have no time to psychoanalyze all these crazy creatures.

CARL JUNG: We are now beyond all that Sigmund. Why can't you recognize an archetype when it hits you over the head with its type?

SIGMUND FREUD: Arche...what?

CARL JUNG: Not your "type" anyway...Symbols!

SIGMUND FREUD: They are what they are...having emerged from our own collective Unconscious Mind.

FYODOR DOSTOYEVSKY: (*Looking over to Beethoven*) Didn't you compose that?

LUDWIG VON BEETHOVEN: Huh? What? Oh, oh, yes, yes...you are referring to my Third?

FYODOR DOSTOYEVSKY: Yes, the one about the "Heroic Man" and how he symbolizes what Jung means.

Beethoven can't hear him.

Napoleon Bonaparte has been lingering around outside the door, debating whether to enter or not. He sees a wild gang in the playground area having a raucous time, but decides to poke his head inside the class just in time to hear Beethoven's comment.

NAPOLEON BONAPARTE: Supposed to be in my honor, wasn't it?

LUDWIG VON BEETHOVEN: Yes, until you mucked it up by declaring yourself Emperor!

NAPOLEON BONAPARTE: It's still my favorite along with your "Ninth."

George Bernard Shaw, or just Bernard Shaw as he preferred, has been in the room since class began. He blurts out:

GEORGE BERNARD SHAW: Where was your "Ode to Joy?"

NAPOLEON BONAPARTE: When I tried to remake history until I discovered it was a mere fable all agreed upon.

WILLIAM SHAKESPEARE: What is past is but a prologue.

ARISTOPHANES: *(Still looking up at the clouds, searching for more birds and now laughing)* You cannot teach a crab to walk straight!

Gautama Buddha has been meditating since the beginning of the class in the back of the room.

GAUTAMA BUDDHA: Sideways is still a path.

PROFESSOR PLATO: We just can't teach class to a class.

Cleopatra strolls elegantly through the door, spraying scented vapor around the room.

CLEOPATRA: All paths lead to me and my ship. I am the Muse of Navigation. My sails are not only purple, but exude a lavender perfume.

JOHN DOWLAND: You could have hired me as your "sound slave" to enliven those passengers riding your nave on their own emotional wave.

CLEOPATRA: Leaving the protective harbors of reason, the Imagination raises its sails.

Friedrich Nietzsche still present but quiet, reawakens.

FRIEDRICH NIETZSCHE: I have said it so many times that if there were no music life would be a serious mistake.

PROFESSOR PLATO: At least you are not hitting us again with your "God is dead" slogan.

FRIEDRICH NIETZSCHE: No slogan, professor, just our modern day tragedy. It is up to us to resurrect ourselves!

JESUS: It is there within. Always has been.

MARY: Once a carpenter always a builder—I am the mother of the idea.

SAMUEL BECKET: How long do we have to wait for this?

THOMAS JEFFERSON: I have already finished our declaration; we are just waiting for everyone to sign on to this adventure.

Mark Twain is dressed in his white suit and seated quietly smoking a corncob pipe. He is just thinking and thinking, and also not thinking.

MARK TWAIN: The only way to get ahead is to get started.

Oscar Wilde in his dandy threads is ready to cause any kind of disturbance.

OSCAR WILDE: Talk about setting the "mark" high, Mr. Twain. Glad to see that you have entered the fray today.

MARK TWAIN: I have been staying away so that this class and schooling in general won't interfere with my education.

OSCAR WILDE: So true! Everything that becomes popular is wrong.

PROFESSOR PLATO: I strongly disagree! We will still have class in my republic.

THOMAS JEFFERSON: Did we all sign on for this? I don't remember that clause in our declaration.

SOCRATES: It is not all in what we write or sign, but in the dialog and what we question.

GEORGE BERNARD SHAW: My education was only interrupted during the time I was in school.

WILLIAM BLAKE: I only really care about cleaning my "doors of perception" and feeding my "tiger of wrath."

Confucius is a stalwart pillar of this class and the whole experience, but as for now...

CONFUCIUS: I am confused.

WILLIAM BLAKE: Because they are wiser than all your horses of instruction?

CONFUCIUS: Such exuberance!

WILLIAM BLAKE: Such beauty!

ARISTOTLE: No great genius without more than a touch of madness.

VASLAV NIJINSKY: I am not mad, just the "faun" in me.

Vincent Van Gogh is pacing in the back of the classroom with a brush and palette in hand.

VINCENT VAN GOGH: Madness!? *(Vincent now pulls out a knife and starts waving it around.)* An eye for an eye, an ear for an ear!

Gauguin is also there wearing his primitive garb, just back from his long stint in Tahiti.

PAUL GAUGUIN: Get ahold of yourself Vincent. You are going to hurt yourself or someone else.

VINCENT VAN GOGH: *(Blurting out halfcrazed)* You are my only friend!

PAUL GAUGUIN: Just be careful! No woman is worth losing an ear over, even when you get an earful.

Voltaire has been seated quietly for the entirety of the class and now feels called to speak up.

VOLTAIRE: Just as a quick reminder, the ear is the avenue to the heart!

Van Gogh now holds up his self-portrait of his bandaged ear.

VINCENT VAN GOGH: Heartless!

Mark Twain now rises, stretches and starts to leave the classroom.

MARK TWAIN: Doesn't this class ever have a recess? I believe now would be a good time for some good old-fashioned fun and games.

PROFESSOR PLATO: We have not gone through the lesson for today yet!

GEORGE BERNARD SHAW: Which would be?

MARK TWAIN: I am heading outside, on to heaven for the climate... leaving this company to hell.

DANTE ALIGHIERI: Did I just hear that familiar word which I have euphemistically referred to as "Inferno?"

Mark Twain, already out the door, did not hear nor take notice.

DANTE ALIGHIERI: I wish I had had Mr Twain's brevity of wit for key lines in my "Divine Comedy"

ARISTOPHANES: The only humor I saw in it was the title, but I, myself, got stuck in "Purgatorio," never quite making it to "Paradiso."

WILLIAM BLAKE: *(interrupting)* "Paradiso" is my fort of comfort.

Mark Twain is already outside the classroom, but we hear his loud voice all the way back inside.

MARK TWAIN: Truth is stranger than fiction...

WILLIAM BLAKE: This road we are on of excess leads straight to the gilded palace of wisdom.

WILLIAM SHAKESPEARE: A fool thinks himself to be wise, but a wise man knows himself to be a fool!

CHARLES DARWIN: Are we wiser now than when we were apes or even birds?

ALBERT EINSTEIN: We never came from them, my dear Charles. The apes are a caricature mistaken for us and the birds are well out of our reach.

WILLIAM BLAKE: Our Imagination is a direct descendent of the birds. We can never soar too high if we use our own "wings."

PROFESSOR PLATO: What about our friend Icarus?

WILLIAM BLAKE: He "waxed" too high when he should have "waned."

Aristophanes laughs heartily at that but, looking around, sees that apparently no one else got it. Just then Aristotle gets up to save the moment.

ARISTOTLE: Of course the wings of Icarus were held together with wax.

ARISTOPHANES: *(Shushing him)* Let 'em figure it out. Isn't that why we are here anyway?

CHARLES DARWIN: I can't see the stars nor even the sun you speak of flying towards.

WOLFGANG AMADEUS MOZART: You need to leave that slime your evolution is stuck in and look up to discover the sublime!

ALBERT EINSTEIN: The only difference between stupidity and genius is that genius has its limits.

ARISTOPHANES: The stupid mistake the clouds for heads and bees for brains!

G.I. GURDJIEFF: There can be no progress or anything learned without discipline being a strict part of the "code of dress."

PROFESSOR PLATO: Are you leading us back to that "hole?"

G.I. GURDJIEFF: We never left it, nor did it leave us. What we cannot dig we cannot do.

FRIEDRICH NIETZSCHE: To do is to learn.

G.I. GURDJIEFF: You have no shovels, so are we stuck in these mental hovels?

PROFESSOR PLATO: Your hole and shovel are not part of my lesson plan!

G.I. GURDJIEFF: Neither is any of the rest of this we have been subjected to here.

GAUTAMA BUDDHA: What we are thinking we become. We are the only ones who can save ourselves.

WILLIAM BLAKE: We make up our own rules or become slave to another man's.

FRIEDRICH NIETZSCHE: Now that I can wrap my head around.

GEORGE SAND: *(Still puffing smoke)* Our own rules? *(She holds up her last pot-boiler novel.)* This is not an example of that. I wrote this only for money, to pay bills...No more! Right, Chopin?!

FREDERICK CHOPIN: I continually break my own set of rules.

FRANZ LISZT: But you completely know what you are doing!

George Sand continues to puff away on her cigar as she stands behind Chopin's chair protectively.

GEORGE SAND: Frederic playing his polonaises and mazurkas brought such tears to my eyes that I thought had none.

FRANZ LISZT: I learned more from the Hungarian folk players than from any teacher of scales and studies. The only true school is in "the touch."

ISADORA DUNCAN: I am touched by all this.

Isadora continues whirling around the classroom barefoot and stops near Beethoven to run her fingers through his still disheveled hair.

ISADORA DUNCAN: Your sonata, "Apassionata," drove me insane as soon as I tried to dance it.

Beethoven looks up at her fondly, hearing everything she has just said.

LUDWIG VON BEETHOVEN: My road runs straight though joy's ode.

ARISTOTLE: If we want to be happy, it depends on us.

John Stuart Mill has arrived, completely determined on being useful to Plato and his classroom objectives.

JOHN STUART MILL: Happiness is basically determined by the amount of "buckets."

MARK TWAIN: *(Back from outside)* I have heard of pass the buck, but never bucket!

JOHN STUART MILL: We are not passing buckets, but filling them with happiness.

FRIEDRICH NIETZSCHE: That is one crazy idea for me.

PROFESSOR PLATO: Please, hear Mr. Mill out!

JOHN STUART MILL: If happiness could be measured in buckets, then the more we have to distribute the greater the happiness for all.

FRIEDRICH NIETZSCHE: No, not for me. No buckets!

JOHN STUART MILL: Ask yourself if you are happy, and you cease to be.

FYODOR DOSTOYEVSKY: Doing nothing will bring no happiness.

LEO TOLSTOY: In the end, writing *War and Peace* only brought me solitude.

FYODOR DOSTOYEVSKY: But the writing—gratitude. You knew what you were doing.

LEO TOLSTOY: My wife enjoyed me reading the galleys to her nightly. I never felt trapped by what I was doing.

FYODOR DOSTOYEVSKY: You are a lucky one. The best way to keep a prisoner from escaping is to make him never know he is in prison.

ALEXANDER PUSHKIN: Ecstasy is a cup full of tea with a piece of cake in the mouth.

Mary has been sitting blissfully all this time near the back of the classroom.

MARY: I am happy just being here!

JESUS: Go ahead, Leonardo! Paint her again. Put yourself back on the map.

LEONARD DAVINCI: I am still working on Nefertiti's bust in profile. I could add Mary to make twin Madonnas, each looking at the other in profile.

Plato looks over at Lao-Tzu, still seated quietly meditating, as if he were on some mountain top or deep within a far-off forest.

PROFESSOR PLATO: Lao! You still with us?

LAO-TZU: Oh, yes! He who knows does not speak. He who speaks does not know.

PROFESSOR PLATO: By the way, how are you doing with your "thousand steps?"

LAO-TZU: Still making that first one over and over again.

SAMUEL BECKET: I am still waiting for my journey to begin. Shakespeare already informed us that "all is prologue until now."

PROFESSOR PLATO: Maybe having this class was a bad idea. I am having some second thoughts on it.

ALBERT EINSTEIN: Why? Because you cannot handle this reality of the "space-time continuum?"

PROFESSOR PLATO: In the Academy of Pythagoras, we heard about this concept through the "Music of the Spheres." All is vibration!

ALBERT EINSTEIN: Space and time by themselves are one-dimensional. The reality is that everything is happening all at once. In a way, like this class you have organized.

VASLAV NIJINSKY: That is what has been driving me mad. I refuse to go on like this. If God were dead and then I became God, it is now already Sunday and my work is done.

Paganini has not stopped with his imaginary violin playing.

NICCOLO PAGANINI: Imagine, I can do all this on only a single string.

With a kind of eerie sound coming at us from outer space, Pythagoras enters wearing his Greek toga. He is carrying his famous "Monochord."

PYTHAGORAS: On the strength of that one string you can see all sound proportions in its length.

FYODOR DOSTOYEVSKY: As I get older as a writer, even when playing on "one string," I can still make those words sing.

WILLIAM SHAKESPEARE: Like wine, the writer improves with age: the fool becomes the sage.

The Fool enters the room, dressed as a medieval jester to play the class clown.

FOOL: Energy is everything! Who can refuse its call?

DANTE ALIGHIERI: Those who don't follow their own star.

Sylvia Plath has been completely invisible like a spirit, dressed all in white. She speaks up only now.

SYLVIA PLATH: When you are insane, you are very busy being insane—all the time.

DANTE ALIGHIERI: In the middle of my journey I came to myself in a dark wood where the straight way was lost. Is that what you are talking about?

SYLVIA PLATH: I took a very deep breath, actually many and then listened to that old bray of my heart. I am. I am. I am.

Rene Descartes arrived even when others doubted he would. He is posed like "The Thinker."

RENE DESCARTES: Traveling is almost like talking with those of other centuries.

GAUTAMA BUDDHA: Walk on! My philosopher friend!

RENE DESCARTES: I think, therefore I am.

JESUS: We are all one body.

Carrying his walking stick and dressed in tattered clothing, Walt Whitman makes his appearance. As he enters, there is a whirlwind that scatters leaves in the classroom.

WALT WHITMAN: And your very flesh can be a great poem.

Just after Whitman, as there is now a chill in the air, Robert Frost enters.

ROBERT FROST: A poet never takes notes. You never take notes in a love affair.

PROFESSOR PLATO: That's enough class! I am so right to not include poets or artists in my Ideal Republic!

Sylvia Plath has now slipped into an almost catatonic trance. She stares into space and talks to no one in particular.

SYLVIA PLATH: Kiss me and you will see how important I am.

Aristophanes, for no particular reason, stands up abruptly and then sits down quickly as if mimicking being called on to answer a question.

Isaac Newton has made a classic entrance, calling the attention of the other students. He then quickly looks up, then down, and then up again.

ISAAC NEWTON: What goes up must come down.

PYTHAGORAS: Mr. Newton, don't make light of all you have fought and stood for.

ISAAC NEWTON: Wasn't it you, my Greek comrade, who once said that "beans have a soul"?

Aristophanes lets out a whooping laugh, as does the Fool.

FOOL: And they call me the Fool!

ARISTOPHANES: You are my favorite here. Don't know why you have been so quiet till now.

PROFESSOR PLATO: Mr. Lao-Tzu, don't say it, please.

Plato then glances over at Buddha to see how he is taking in everything.

LAO-TZU: Silence is a source...

PROFESSOR PLATO: *(Interrupting Lao-Tzu)* We know. Your steps and your journey.

LAO-TZU: The wise traveler has no intent on arriving.

ROBERT FROST: *(Blurting out)* Poetry is where the emotion has...

Isadora suddenly swoops in front of Robert and Lao-Tzu.

ISADORA DUNCAN: Me!

ROBERT FROST: ...thought and the thought has found...

ISADORA DUNCAN: Me!

ROBERT FROST: Words!

Plato, obviously annoyed, glances over at Pythagoras, who is humming rather loudly.

PYTHAGORAS: There is geometry in the humming of the strings. There is music in the spacing of the…

Paganini cuts in with a snippet of his wild bowing and music.

PYTHAGORAS: …Spheres.

Archimedes has entered, looking well-balanced, but seeming to have some weighty concern about him.

ARCHIMEDES: Eureka! But…have we really found it?

GAUTAMA BUDDHA: Be not the seeker, let it come to you.

JESUS: Amen! Be the seeker of yourself.

ARISTOPHANES: Keep it simple! Just do what your wife says!

ISADORA DUNCAN: You could well be the very first feminist, Aristophanes!

ARISTOPHANES: Is that what you call it? I am just trying to stay out of trouble.

PROFESSOR PLATO: Any of you change your mind about the class?

Hippocrates has been there a while, in his typical Greek toga with a healthy air about him.

HIPPOCRATES: So far, it has been about "nothing," which is fine. For the body, "nothing" is also a good remedy.

ARISTOPHANES: Love that! I feel at home with anything, anywhere that I can prosper.

PROFESSOR PLATO: All of us here are responsible for the success of our class adventure.

CLEOPATRA: It has been strange and also terrible, which I most welcome. I am in love with luxury, yet happily despise comfort.

Richard Wagner has finally showed up, with the wind now blowing harder outside. He overhears Cleopatra's remark and, never feeling any struggle for words, responds.

RICHARD WAGNER: The only one I see comfortable here is our one and only muse, Isadora.

LEONARD DAVINCI: At the moment, Nefertiti is our current object of adoration.

MICHELANGELO: Always the star.

LEONARD DAVINCI: The one I was born under I have striven to become.

PROFESSOR PLATO: We are here to challenge this zone of comfort. In a way, what Cleopatra says is right.

Wagner, now struggling to catch up but not wanting to agree to anything, replies to Plato.

RICHARD WAGNER: We are not all on the same page as you, Plato.

Plato looks over at Wagner, dressed luxuriously in a fur coat, with an air of disdain.

RICHARD WAGNER: I've never been so inspired to write music and so deeply in debt. I actually agreed to come here when I got word of your class to pass the hat.

ARISTOPHANES: *(Howling now)* Came to us for money!?

FOOL: I am not so easy to fool, but that's a good one.

Virgil was one of the first to arrive and has been completely silent up till now. He now starts to speak, and then decides to keep quiet. The Fool notices his hesitation and turns to Virgil.

FOOL: Well?!

VIRGIL: Fortune sides with those who dare. I can applaud Mr. Wagner.

FOOL: For some, their gods are in the twilight and for others, their "sun" is rising.

GAUTAMA BUDDHA: The gods are all fond of a joke, wise fool.

GEORGE BERNARD SHAW: This class has the atmosphere of "summer school." I see no interruption in "my education."

SIGMUND FREUD: There is a lot to swallow here.

CARL JUNG: You should be fine. Didn't you once confide in me regarding your mouth fetish?

GAUTAMA BUDDHA: *(Appearing more animated)* Uncommonly so. One swallow does not make a summer.

SOLOMON: A true fool is wise in his eyes.

FOOL: Hell is empty now because its devils are here.

WILLIAM SHAKESPEARE: Hey, that's my line, you fool!

PROFESSOR PLATO: Though you have all received the call to come here to assemble, there is still time to refuse. No funds were transacted.

MARK TWAIN: I like to keep my mouth shut and let others think that I am a fool than to open it and remove all doubt.

FOOL: Even I could not have come up with that, and this is my area of expertise!

GAUTAMA BUDDHA: The present is our present.

JOAN OF ARC: I fear I was born to do this. When you act, God acts.

PROFESSOR PLATO: You are present and accounted for Joan. I hear no refusal.

JOAN OF ARC: It is time for me to act. The Hundred Years' War calls me to battle.

CLEOPATRA: You are strangely beautiful, Joan.

GAUTAMA BUDDHA: She is a saint making her own happiness.

Joan's horse without warning bursts into the room, and Joan jumps on it and is gone. Nefertiti now turns away from her profile after a long while and looks at Leonardo.

NEFERTITI: I am an unsolved mystery. Wouldn't you have preferred to have captured Joan with immortal style of precision technique?

LEONARD DAVINCI: It is your dark mystery that haunts me. I intend to solve it with my brush.

Nefertiti reverts back to her profile pose for Leonardo to continue. Suddenly the room gets very quiet as everyone seems to be looking at something going on in the very center of the space.

PROFESSOR PLATO: What do we have here?

Franz Kafka is on the floor in a ball, seemingly imitating some kind of insect in a stage of metamorphosis.

CHARLES DARWIN: Is it trying to evolve?

FRANZ KAFKA: Just be quiet and listen...simply wait.

SAMUEL BECKET: Hey, I like you already.

FRANZ KAFKA: ...Be still. You need not leave the room. The world will offer itself to you...roll in ecstasy at your feet!

Kafka starts to roll and move as if trying desperately to open "insect wings."

MARK TWAIN: I said it before and I'll say it again: Truth is stranger than fiction.

CHARLES DARWIN: I get it! You always thought "I" was nuts.

FRANZ KAFKA: God gives us nuts, but he does not crack them.

ARISTOPHANES: Forget my women on strike. This is good stuff here. I think I was born a few hundred years too early.

FOOL: We have no choice but to laugh.

Galileo Galilei has been weighing in off to the side of the class, trying to stay out of his own way.

GALILEO GALILEI: ...And yet it moves when senses fail us.

FOOL: This is all nonsense here.

GALILEO GALILEI: Franz, you have spent too long looking down. We should all take your advice, Plato... *(Looking nervously at the still hunching Kafka)* ...and start our studies with mathematics.

PROFESSOR PLATO: That is the first solid thing I have heard all morning.

CHARLES DARWIN: Let Mr. Kafka continue on with his transformation. Each one's happiness is relative.

ALBERT EINSTEIN: Just as my general relativity predicted. The spacetime around our Earth would be not only warped but also twisted by the planet's rotation.

VASLAV NIJINSKY: That is exactly how I feel when I dance—twisted in my own states of mad rotation.

JOHANN SEBASTIAN BACH: It is all movement—all a dance.

LUDWIG VON BEETHOVEN: Never doubted that for a moment.

FOOL: Take a chance to enter the whirling garden of the dance.

JESUS: That is where I meditate best.

MARY: In the garden?

JESUS: In the dancing garden.

PROFESSOR PLATO: Where are our true men of today?

Plato starts to look around at each class member, searching for a reply. Finally Nietzsche stands up abruptly.

FRIEDRICH NIETZSCHE: Generally the true man you refer to, Herr Professor Plato, wants two things: danger and play.

WOLFGANG AMADEUS MOZART: Interesting concept.

FRIEDRICH NIETZSCHE: For that reason, he wants woman as his most dangerous plaything.

LUDWIG VON BEETHOVEN: The Eternal Muse.

FRIEDRICH NIETZSCHE: They make the higher just higher.

LUDWIG VON BEETHOVEN: And what about...

FRIEDRICH NIETZSCHE: The lower?...more Frequent!

There has been a rather simple and quiet woman present since the class began. She has brought an apple for Professor Plato, but until now has not given it to him. It is the first woman, Eve!

EVE: I am the bookends of your day—both morning and EVEning.

FRIEDRICH NIETZSCHE: I am the "one," oddly enough.

EVE: Even I too.

PROFESSOR PLATO: Ultimately, this is what this class is all about: that one-two punch.

The four women, Nefertiti, Isadora, Mary and Eve, now assume a temporary chorus.

CHORUS: We are right—always!

PROFESSOR PLATO: At least one thing has been decided upon today.

ARISTOPHANES: Are we to conclude, then, that woman is here to be man's mentor?

PROFESSOR PLATO: I believe that it might be time to take that break that Mr. Twain was all excited about some time ago.

Aristotle now directs a question straight at Shakespeare.

ARISTOTLE: Have we in fact finished what you term: The Prologue?

WILLIAM SHAKESPEARE: That was referring to life—out there!

RENE DESCARTES: There is a separation then, but not mind and body as I thought but...

DANTE ALIGHIERI: The secret is to act to get things done.

RENE DESCARTES: Yes, but it is rather in here AND out there.

Mark Twain has already reentered and now motions to all of them.

MARK TWAIN: Right now is the moment for "out there" to come about.

II

The Courtyard
Ancient School of Dialog and Learning

The classroom's doors are flung wide open with Twain leading. They all make their way into the courtyard exercise area of the Ancient School of Dialog and Learning. There is another group of "students" lurking our there. Who are they? Why weren't they invited in? Or maybe they were but chose to stay away.

Leonardo, the most curious, approaches the group holding Nefertitti's hand and carrying the canvas he is planning to continue working on with the help of natural lighting.

Nero, wearing the laurel wreath of an Emperor, is reaching for something inside his long Roman-style toga. Many of Plato's students have hesitated to go too near this band of "outsiders" on the opposite side of the courtyard area. Nero now looks over at Machiavelli and strikes a long wooden match.

NERO: Think we should burn it down?

MACHIAVELLI: *(Looking excited)* Bunch of time-wasters!

NERO: Wish I could have seen that ancient library of Alexandria burn.

MACHIAVELLI: Must have been quite a sight and quite sad.

Nero is still fiddling with his long matchstick and debating in his mind as to what to do.

NERO: Yes, I would have given ten Christians to have witnessed it first hand.

Machiavelli glances over at Nero with a disapproving look.

MACHIAVELLI: Guess it is better for you to be feared than loved if you can't have both.

Leon Trotsky now comes forward to where the others are standing.

LEON TROTSKY: My revolutionary art is nothing like they are babbling about inside their classroom.

Adolf Hitler is also among them, milling around apparently with nothing to do. He strolls up to stand next to Trotsky.

ADOLF HITLER: If my first art teacher had not failed me so badly I would not be so mad. Now it is time to use words to build bridges into unexplored regions.

Joseph Stalin is also amongst them and looking as stern as ever.

JOSEPH STALIN: Was it as bad as all that?

ADOLF HITLER: Those damn 'Modernists!" Anyone who sees a sky green and fields blue ought to be sterilized!

NERO: When the Christians entered the arena, were they singing?

Nero has looked over at Pontius Pilatus who is also among the gang.

PONTIUS PILATUS: You would have known what to do with Jesus, who they called Christ.

NERO: Yeah, as long as he could sing!

PONTIUS PILATUS: He kept on claiming to be king.

Out of the blue, not green, Jesus appears in a vision of light before them. They all take a step back in both surprise and shock.

JESUS: *You* said so!

PONTIUS PILATUS: You live!

JESUS: Not in your kingdom!

NERO: Nor in my arena. Way too much light!

Nero tries desperately to shield his face, as the light is obviously causing him pain.

JESUS: I am for those who see.

Jesus disappears instantly even before the other students from inside Plato's class could notice he had gone there.

PONTIUS PILATUS: I am innocent, having long since washed my hands of him. What a trouble-maker.

Hitler in the background has been listening to the discussion and jumps in.

ADOLF HITLER: And they say that we're the problem. Hah! *(Shaking his head)* The day of the individual and their own personal happiness has passed. It's over!

Napoleon has been seen with both groups—Plato's class and with the gang of "outsiders."

NAPOLEON BONAPARTE: We need their religion more than they do. It is what keeps the poor from outright murdering the rich.

Karl Marx has a large copy of "Das Kapital" under his arm and has been trying to get these thugs to look at it.

KARL MARX: Their road to hell is paved with the best of intentions.

ADOLF HITLER: Didn't you also once say something about religion as their opium?

Before Marx can reply Napoleon chimes in.

NAPOLEON BONAPARTE: As long as they are drugged with it and believe they are doing right, we are saved.

KARL MARX: Don't care much for your style, Herr Bonaparte. Beethoven was probably right to strike your name from his third symphony.

NAPOLEON BONAPARTE: How did you find THAT out?

KARL MARX: We had a beer together one night when I happened to be passing through Bonn.

ADOLF HITLER: I heard he drank a lot, but still would have liked to cross paths with him.

NAPOLEON BONAPARTE: He would not have heard any of your tirades, no matter how much you gesticulated as if in a game of charades.

KARL MARX: The modern history of capital dates from the creation in the 16th century of a world-embracing commerce together with a world-embracing market.

Mao Zedong is also there, amongst them in the background but now has something to contribute eyeing Marx's large volume of "Das Kapital."

MAO ZEDONG: I have always preached that reading too many books is harmful. We never really want to wake the tiger, just poke at him with a very long stick.

ADOLF HITLER: Only one is necessary: mine!

MAO ZEDONG: Was it ghost-written?

ADOLF HITLER: What are you implying?

MAO ZEDONG: I knew you once once tried your hand at painting but...

ADOLF HITLER: *(Getting crazy now)* But what?! Hate is more lasting than dislike. Like it or leave it!

MACHIAVELLI: They say you have perfected the "great lie."

ADOLF HITLER: If I tell you a big enough lie, and tell it frequently enough, it will be believed.

At that moment, the sky outside where they are all congregated in the schoolyard darkens with a huge thundercloud. A well-dressed "gentleman" appears out of nowhere in their midst, wearing black velvet gloves and a long satin coat-and-cape blend with a crimson interior lining. It is none other than Satan himself.

SATAN: I am loving the energy here, as well as this cool shadow in place of a much overrated rainbow. It is a very refreshing break from those fires I have just come from.

ADOLF HITLER: You look so familiar, but I just can't seem to place you.

SATAN: I also dictate—not to a secretary but to hordes of devils and demons.

NERO: Let me guess. I believe I may have caught a glimpse of you during one of my cithara concerts. Those damn Christians always sang louder when they saw I was playing.

SATAN: What a show, and you must have been proud of your lions too.

JOSEPH STALIN: Satin, glad you could join us. The Pope also asked for an invitation, but didn't have enough legions to qualify.

SATAN: Oh yes, the Pope. We're on again, off again. You just never know which team he is batting for.

ADOLF HITLER: Gotta love your style. Do you mind if I call you the satin Satan?

SATAN: No, not at all. I have surely been called so much worse. Actually, the worse the better: it helps me live up to my reputation. It is all about image, no matter what side you are on.

ADOLF HITLER: Though I am not French, I love occupying myself in Paris reading Voltaire.

NAPOLEON BONAPARTE: This is getting better and better.

ADOLF HITLER: Voltaire taught, when at war to hold a pen, and that if you are clever you'll never be punished, even if tyrannical.

Hitler now holds up his pen with a Nazi symbol on it. Shakespeare, on the other side of the courtyard sees the raised pen and points to it for Dante to also see it.

WILLIAM SHAKESPEARE: It looks like some kind of writing utensil, but so different from my quill.

JESUS: That gentleman dressed to kill looks more than slightly familiar.

Satan sees Jesus eyeing him and tips his black, velvet-rimmed hat in his direction. Jesus now looks back at his friend, Buddha, and continues speaking to him.

JESUS: I am tempted to go have a word with that man.

Buddha, who always has his back, steps up to Jesus.

GAUTAMA BUDDHA: That overly dressed "gentleman" who just made eye contact with you worries me.

JESUS: I am sure we have already met. The question is where?

GAUTAMA BUDDHA: Just be still on this one. Let him make the first move. Look at who he is with over there!

Mark Twain has approached the two and joins in the conversation, followed by Walt Whitman.

MARK TWAIN: Your major source of inspiration?

WALT WHITMAN: It was what my publisher referred to as a minor work.

MARK TWAIN: Which?

WALT WHITMAN: Grass!

MARK TWAIN: Oh, I get it. Written on the "leaves," or sheaves of paper.

WALT WHITMAN: But I ended up smoking them. What a surprise when my first edition sold out.

MARK TWAIN: I had to do it the hard way—doing lecture tours.

Satan is still looking over at Jesus and now yells out to him.

SATAN: I am here for you. Just look—the picture of success! You could have all this too!

Satan twirls around to show off his fancy and sophisticated garb to Jesus. Jesus merely listens and looks on.

SATAN: Just follow my steps and all that you can imagine is yours.

GAUTAMA BUDDHA: Just ignore his taunting. He is trying to show off in front of his cohorts.

Suddenly, Jesus realizes just who he is.

JESUS: Satan!!

Satan is now gesturing that all that gang is under his command and motions to Jesus to come and join. Then he begins to laugh deeply and heartily. Jesus immediately loses interest and turns back to his own classmates. Alexander the Great is now looking over at Satan.

ALEXANDER THE GREAT: I have already conquered "his" world that he claims to "own." Just ignore him, Jesus.

JESUS: It's a no-brainer—"his kingdom" or my soul? And "his kingdom" is not even all his.

ALEXANDER THE GREAT: I can see some of the other conquerers in their gang. Just who are they?

JESUS: Disregard them. It is not just the bread to feed, but the seeds of the word to plant that we need.

There is some more commotion in the schoolyard as Ernest Hemingway and F. Scott Fitzgerald have shown up for Plato's class and join the others in the yard. Hemingway is talking and laughing with Fitzgerald.

ERNEST HEMINGWAY: The best way to find out if you can trust somebody is to trust them.

Hemingway is in a gregarious mood and pulls a flask of rum from inside his coat, takes a long swig, then turns to Fitzgerald.

ERNEST HEMINGWAY: Look who we have here, Fitzgerald!

Hemingway motions with his flask to the members of Plato's class in their recess.

F. SCOTT FITZGERALD: Who are they?

ERNEST HEMINGWAY: We, who are the geniuses, are forced to drink to put up with these fools.

Plato, who has also left the classroom for a break, scrutinizes the two writers who had arrived late and is informed that they are from the "Lost Generation." Shakespeare comes up to Plato's side to talk.

PROFESSOR PLATO: Not sure just who they are. Anyway, they are late and it looks like they are half drunk.

WILLIAM SHAKESPEARE: At first glance, I'm not sure where they'd fit: comedy or tragedy?

ARISTOPHANES: Doesn't matter. When you're lost, you're lost.

Just coming now behind Hemingway and Fitzgerald arrives Pablo Picasso. Picasso comes over to where the painter Raphael is standing, unaware of just who he is. Raphael moves closer to Leonardo, who had just set up his easel outdoors in the courtyard to continue painting Nefertiti. Raphael pulls out his latest sketches for Leonardo to see.

RAPHAEL: When I paint or sketch I am not thinking.

LEONARD DAVINCI: Your Sistine Madonna far out paces anything done by Michelangelo.

RAPHAEL: Let it go, Leonardo. It does not become you.

LEONARD DAVINCI: Who's that short, stocky guy coming towards us.

RAPHAEL: Never seen him before. Don't think he would have thought much of my "Three Graces."

LEONARD DAVINCI: You no doubt once shared the same muse but now...

Picasso comes closer and speaks just as a wind kicks up all across the schoolyard.

PABLO PICASSO: The wind seems to be getting stronger all the time.

RAPHAEL: Then you start to feel it in your face.

Raphael looks back at Leonardo sensing something very familiar about Picasso.

PABLO PICASSO: I vaguely remember something about you. Aren't you that "Madonna man?"

LEONARD DAVINCI: How did you come up with that?

PABLO PICASSO: My father had me study the Renaissance in my earlier years.

RAPHAEL: Yes, I painted a few.

PABLO PICASSO: Good artists copy, great artists steal.

LEONARD DAVINCI: Now I remember. You're the one who took all those years to learn how to paint like a child.

PABLO PICASSO: It just came to me. You're Raphael, the god of my youth.

Raphael shows no reaction to the off-handed compliment. He looks over at the gang of outsiders, then back at Hemingway and Fitzgerald.

RAPHAEL: Those your people?

PABLO PICASSO: They call us "lost." I don't know where I found them—guess it was Paris.

In pure reverie recollecting, Picasso runs his hand over his totally bald head.

PABLO PICASSO: We all met at the house of Ms. Stein.

Hemingway strolls over still waving his flask around and overhears Picasso.

ERNEST HEMINGWAY: That "rose is a rose is a rose" lady. *(He laughs drunkenly.)*

F. SCOTT FITZGERALD: Who are those guys on the opposite side of the courtyard?

PROFESSOR PLATO: We don't really know. They were not asked to come to our school. They just showed up today.

F. SCOTT FITZGERALD: Pretty scary looking gang!

ERNEST HEMINGWAY: Relax "Fitz." Nothing we can't handle. Why remember...

F. SCOTT FITZGERALD: Not now, "Papa," spare us.

We hear a lot of yelling and arguing from across the yard. Picasso appears to be talking now to himself as Raphael is distracted by the "gang of outsiders" disturbance.

PABLO PICASSO: All children are artists. The problem is how to remain one as you grow up.

Maximilian Robespierre has arrived across the way and is now engaged in a heated discussion.

ROBESPIERRE: I have said it once and will say it again—the king must die so that the country can live.

Napoleon walks back and forth between the two groups.

NAPOLEON BONAPARTE: Never really believed that.

ROBESPIERRE: Traitor! Tyrant! Pity is treason!

NERO: Where's my violin, I mean cithara, now that I really need it. Ahhhh, the joys of the arena.

ERNEST HEMINGWAY: I believe we are in for some adventure here. Where did I leave my notebook?!

F. SCOTT FITZGERALD: And I a quick drink, where is that flask, Papa?

Caligula, that blood thirsty psychopath Roman Emperor, has also surfaced in their gang and enters the fray as he yells out.

CALIGULA: Let them hate me so long as they fear me!

NERO: You took those words right out of my mouth.

Julius Caesar strides down the very middle of the yard with an air that all is his.

JULIUS CAESAR: We have not to fear anything, except fear itself.

PABLO PICASSO: We do or not do all depending on our level of fear.

F. SCOTT FITZGERALD: I have always been envious of your enormous output. How do you do it?

PABLO PICASSO: I am always doing what I don't know how to do. That's how I get so much done.

ERNEST HEMINGWAY: Oh, so that's your secret. I have never seen you hit the bottle.

PABLO PICASSO: When I get down I work. That's my real drug. A creative junkie. I HAVE to have it!

They are interrupted by a huge trumpeting sound. It is Hannibal arriving on an elephant.

HANNIBAL: I will either find a way or make one. I have no interest in understanding sheep, only eating them!

JULIUS CAESAR: I came, I saw, I conquered!

HANNIBAL: You, Julius, have inspired me my entire life. I had your words in my mind when I took those elephants over the Swiss Alps.

ERNEST HEMINGWAY: How majestic and powerful you look atop your elephant. Better to be here than at a bull-fight. Who put all this together anyway?

ARISTOPHANES: That would be our headmaster: Professor Plato!

ERNEST HEMINGWAY: Plato...Plato...hmmm. Yes, the classics. Which was that Dialog that spoke on "Quality?"

PROFESSOR PLATO: That would be "Phaedrus," Mr. Hemingway. It has been referred to as one of my Greek pillars of thought.

More commotion in the yard interrupts them once again. Grigori Rasputin is causing a disturbance in the midst of that gang of outsiders.

GRIGORI RASPUTIN: None of you, I imagine, are aware of my power to sway you.

JOSEPH STALIN: What are you all excited about? Who are you anyway?

GRIGORI RASPUTIN: How could you not know?

Dostoyevsky crosses the yard now with his notes in his hand and heads right up to Stalin.

FYODOR DOSTOYEVSKY: Stalin, you know absolutely nothing of Mother Russia!

JOSEPH STALIN: You, Mr. Dostoyevsky were damn lucky to have survived that firing squad. Your guardian angel definitely worked overtime on that cold morning in Siberia!

FYODOR DOSTOYEVSKY: Nevertheless here I am. Siberia!! *(He points at Rasputin.)* He is the mad Siberian monk who ran the whole show in the Romanov court. You fascist dictators know nothing of our own history.

GRIGORI RASPUTIN: All the women fell at my feet. They could not resist my powers!

JOSEPH STALIN: Which were?

GRIGORI RASPUTIN: I am a healer! I weathered the wastes of Siberia making my way to St Petersburg on foot.

FYODOR DOSTOYEVSKY: It was there, Mr. Stalin, that he quickly caught the attention of our Russian high society.

JOSEPH STALIN: Yes, that does ring some "orthodox bell."

FYODOR DOSTOYEVSKY: A former serf who mingled with the elite of St. Petersburg.

GRIGORI RASPUTIN: And cured many of their bizarre ailments when I wasn't running after the court ladies to court. *(He lets out a bellow of laughter.)*

ADOLF HITLER: We could have made good German use of your mystical powers.

Rasputin suddenly goes into a frenzy of death defying yells and holds his throat and guts while screaming out.

GRIGORI RASPUTIN: This was what it was like when they poisoned me with cyanide, shot me three times, beat me badly and then threw me into the icy Malaya Nevka river. I was given up for dead but...

Trotsky cuts in not containing himself a moment longer.

LEON TROTSKY: The story goes, Joseph, that he froze in the icy river...and preserved through time, resurrected with his memory of all that happened intact.

JOSEPH STALIN: Unbelievable!

LEON TROTSKY: Who was it here who said "reality is stranger than fiction?"

We switch back to the other side of the schoolyard, where Plato is still with his class.

MARK TWAIN: Now that is what I call having fun in the schoolyard. *(Looking over at Rasputin's antics)* All this would have been a normal ho-hum day on the Mississippi.

Archimedes suddenly comes alive with something to say.

ARCHIMEDES: Never discount our power as inventors and scientists. Give me a lever long enough and a fulcrum on which to place it, and I shall move the world.

PROFESSOR PLATO: Why didn't you ever want to contribute to our class inside?

ARCHIMEDES: I had no leverage. Too many prima donnas.

A morning-glory flies close to the tree where Walt Whitman is leaning against it writing.

WALT WHITMAN: *(Yelling out)* You satisfy me more than all the philosophies and metaphysics of books.

For some reason this word "books" starts to echo and reverberate all the way across the yard, increasing in volume till it reaches the sharp ear of Mao.

MAO ZEDONG: Books!!...Wish I could have been there along with you, Nero, to hear the crackle of the library fire in Alexandria. Books and highly treasured scrolls aflame, and look at me, an illiterate peasant who can barely sign his own name.

Rasputin calms a bit but still displays that haunting stare of one very crazed Siberian monk. Trotsky glances over at him.

LEON TROTSKY: You needed no mystical book to work your magic, just the eyes of a mad visionary.

MAO ZEDONG: As a brother of our creed, how do you view art, anyway, Leon, if I can call you that?

LEON TROTSKY: By all means, Chairman. I believe that art is not really a mirror, but a hammer: it does not reflect nor ape, but attempts to shape.

MAO ZEDONG: Too late to add that to my "Little Red Book" as it has become known. It's not a bad book for an "illiterate."

LEON TROTSKY: Think of a sledgehammer that breaks glass but cannot forge steel—now you get the feel?

Trotsky picks up an imaginary sledgehammer and begins to flail it around.

JOSEPH STALIN: You cannot make revolutions with silk gloves. Hey, who is that coming our way?

Hannibal dismounts from his elephant and approaches the gang of outsiders.

HANNIBAL: For fifteen years, I held my ground in hostile territory. What have any of you accomplished?

Plato has been listening intently to them for the past few moments.

PROFESSOR PLATO: It is the most difficult of all to find the "accomplished man."

ADOLF HITLER: *(Sneering and somehow hearing Plato's remark)* I always accomplish what I set out to do!

Plato goes silent as Hannibal stares him down.

ADOLF HITLER: At least in the beginning.

JOSEPH STALIN: You have a short memory, Adolf. You could not handle our winter, remember?

ADOLF HITLER: I have always had a soft spot for London—my downfall.

JOSEPH STALIN: Is that the truth? You, yourself, have just said that great liars are great magicians.

ADOLF HITLER: I still believe it all comes down to the magical act. Can you pull it off or not?

Still dressed in his medieval clown costume, the Fool goes back and forth between the two groups.

FOOL: And they STILL persist in calling me the Fool!

Plato glances over at Socrates who is standing under the shade of the one tree in the yard.

SOCRATES: I still know nothing.

PROFESSOR PLATO: That is nothing new, my "teacher."

This extended break from Plato's class gave the women a chance to reunite among themselves, isolated from the two opposing groups in the courtyard. Their meeting had been prompted by the sudden and completely unexpected arrival of the Trung Sisters from Vietnam, riding on two more elephants. Hannibal, an elephant man himself, was impressed when seeing them arrive.

HANNIBAL: Wow! Who knew my entry could have been upstaged!

The Trung sisters were immediately followed by the arrival of Helen of Troy. She had missed the class, but was here for the women's special class meeting. She appropriately came wearing a crown in the shape of a ship.

HELEN OF TROY: Everyone knows what effect I had on sea-faring vessels.

CLEOPATRA: They were not launched in vain. Your beauty is breathtaking!

ISADORA DUNCAN: All artists are not born into the "royalty vine," but need to create their own "bloodline."

George Sand is still puffing away with her own charm, while watching her "sisters" assemble and verbally arm.

GEORGE SAND: We are our own class.

MARY: Where the word "class" originated from.

Nefertiti has worked her way away from the clutches of Leonardo and his obsession with her as his new ideal model to come and join the women.

NEFERTITI: There is nothing that is ranked higher than our dancers in diaphanous robes moving their bodies freely in both sensual dance and in deep mystical trance.

Isadora continues dancing as if illustrating Nefertitti's words.

GEORGE SAND: Elegant, graceful and at all times ever tasteful.

ISADORA DUNCAN: We can run, leap, do pirouettes and even bend into full wheels...

Hannibal looks on with great interest as more amazing women are arriving. He recognizes Delilah now appearing carrying a small loom and displaying her infamous seven braids.

DELILAH: I am not afraid to say for all to hear that it has not been easy being married to the strongest man in the world.

Elizabeth I has also made a discreet entry and comes to stand next to Delilah. Catherine the Great is also among these most powerful women the world has seen.

CATHERINE THE GREAT: Elizabeth, I had no expectations of meeting you here. I have always wanted you to see my vast collection of Art!

ELIZABETH I: *(Pointing to Catherine)* Delilah, this is a woman to reckon with, who could easily handle your Samson.

Hildegard is still singing in a cappella as she approaches the group of women leaders.

HILDEGARD VON BINGEM: Though I don't consider myself royalty, my head tells me I possess equal authority.

CATHERINE THE GREAT: *(Looking entertained)* Why was I so concerned about adding to Russia's coffers and territorial expansion?

ELIZABETH I: Right here we are experiencing true expansion!

NEFERTITI: Of the spirit!

HILDEGARD VON BINGEM: The soul dances.

MARY: At last!

Salome has also been called to come, and looks on approvingly.

SALOME: If i could do it all over, I would not have had his head but tried to save him from the dead.

ELIZABETH I: One man with a head on his shoulders is worth a dozen without.

CATHERINE THE GREAT: This is a headline in ink for my French friend, Voltaire, who never had time nor patience to read my own "column" written on everything I think.

MARY: This is OUR news now that cannot even be written, just danced.

The Trung Sisters have by now dismounted from their great elephants and joined the rest of the women.

TRUNG SISTERS: *(Speaking in unison)* None of the sixty-five citadels we captured from Chinese control was as exciting for us as just being here. The true warrior ultimately is the dancer!

ISADORA DUNCAN: We have here, in you two, our own version of Hannibal. What are your names?

TRUNG SISTERS: The Trung Sisters! We got wind of your meeting during our travels. When you speak "elephant" nothing is out of your reach!

They both laugh as they playfully imitate the walk and reach of the elephant's trunk.

GEORGE SAND: *(Finally putting down her cigar)* A pity Marco Polo never crossed your path—he seems to have seen everything in the Far East, even picking up your math.

TRUNG SISTERS: We heard of his legendary exploits and how he once dined with the infamous Genghis Khan, not the grandson, Kubla Khan.

At that precise moment another exotic stranger arrives to add further excitement to this burgeoning group of power women. It is Penthesilea, the great Amazon warrior. She is carrying a mallet and wearing a Greek tunic with one of her breasts bare.

PENTHESILEA: Though you may have heard of our Amazon tribe of women, you may not know me by name. I am Penthesilea, the original queen of the Amazons.

ELIZABETH I: There is always room for one more queen. I have heard many stories about you and your Amazon sisters blazing through the Greeks like lightning.

PENTHESILEA: Achilles and I fell in love at first sight. Two mights made a wrong. *(She laughs at her own little joke.)*

MARY: What tragedy befell you?

PENTHESILEA: His sword stuck at the same moment as his love struck.

ISADORA DUNCAN: How tragic!

PENTHESILEA: He thought me dead, but I reawakened from the blow the following day. His sword had hit my concealed breastplate on the side where I wield my bow. His real tragedy was he never knew, nor found out later.

NEFERTITI: Leonardo would be inspired to paint you I have no doubt.

ISADORA DUNCAN: I am the Hellenic dancer, so he just might get around to me sooner or later.

Very unexpected, Clara Schumann makes her belated arrival. She too had missed out on Plato's first class.

CLARA SCHUMANN: Music is in the air. I am painfully missing my beloved piano!

GEORGE SAND: Oh yeah, that is hilarious. You mean the one that only your husband, Robert, played on?

CLARA SCHUMANN: I guess not too many know the story.

ISADORA DUNCAN: Only one piano in the house and it was his, right?

CLARA SCHUMANN: I could only compose on it when he left home in that phase of his mad reveries. He'd be gone—out of his mind for days on end.

GEORGE SAND: Chopin told me all about it. How sad!

CLARA SCHUMANN: It was only when he was mad that the keys freed up for me.

MARY: The real battlefield is in the hearts of men and women, each fighting in hopes the other might yield.

CATHERINE THE GREAT: My life of lust was an open secret through which I lost all my trust.

HILDEGARD VON BINGEM: My heart scored my passion in music I learned in my own fashion.

ELIZABETH I: In fashion!

Now we hear more noise and confusion from that gang of outsiders on the other side of the yard. It was none other than

Satan himself, again, who was stirring things up. Plato got involved to quiet things down.

SATAN: Who in the hell are you anyway. So familiar!

Satan is looking over at Nostradamus, who is wandering around seemingly lost in his own trance. He carries his own book entitled, Centuries.

NOSTRADAMUS: You yourself, Satan, shall commit so many evil acts, my Infernal Prince! Almost undoing the entire world by your own hand alone.

SATAN: How do you speak with this authority directly to me?

NOSTRADAMUS: This is your third and last time on the planet. Please enjoy your last hurrah!

Satan throws off his black top hat, whirls around and flings open his cloak to reveal his crimson velvet lining.

SATAN: You say it's my last time. Don't you think I know it?!

Elephants, nervous, start trumpeting and raising up their front legs in agitation. Joan of Arc suddenly reappears on her horse displaying her own dramatic cape.

NOSTRADAMUS: The present time, together with the past, shall be judged by a great humorist!

The Fool, always nearby, hears his cue and responds with his clue.

FOOL: I have judged before and will do so again if called. Seriously, I am not to be taken seriously. Don't be fooled!

NOSTRADAMUS: Sham liberty shall be proclaimed everywhere!

SATAN: *(Howling with laughter)* My plan exactly!!

Jesus and Buddha look on calmly, incredibly serene in these circumstances. Mary leaves her group of women and approaches her son's side.

MARY: Is this the one who asked you to follow him? *(She motions towards Satan.)*

JESUS: Yes Mother. Is it easy for you to see how simple my choice was?

Genghis Khan is aroused over with the gang and moves up next to Satan.

GENGHIS KHAN: Remember, you have no companions but your own shadow.

Back with Plato's group, Isaac Newton gazes upward overhead.

ISAAC NEWTON: I can calculate the motion of the planets, but not the madness of people.

He stares over at Satan.

MAHATMA GANDHI: Live now as if you were to die tomorrow!

Plato's class has now regrouped and headed over across to the gang of outsiders to form a semicircle near them like an impromptu audience.

PROFESSOR PLATO: Looks like a new "class" is about to begin here outside.

Beethoven is lost in his own creative rage, apparently oblivious of his immediate surroundings.

LUDWIG VON BEETHOVEN: I will seize fate by the throat!

WINSTON CHURCHILL: When you are traveling through hell, keep going.

Descartes just shakes his head as he continues to observe this "Satan show."

RENE DESCARTES: An optimist sees light where there is none, but why must the pessimist always run to blow it out?

Hitler is also now getting riled up and stares blankly at Nostradamus.

ADOLF HITLER: Suppose you're gonna say that you predicted my rise too…

NOSTRADAMUS: All I said was that a young child would be born of poor people from the depths of the west of Europe and his tongue would seduce a great troop.

ADOLF HITLER: Ahhhh yes!

NOSTRADAMUS: And his fame will increase moving towards the East.

ADOLF HITLER: By the way it's "Hitler," not "Hisler," unless you are confusing me with another one of your "visions."

NOSTRADAMUS: *(Replying casually)* Just another Antichrist.

GAUTAMA BUDDHA: *(Still looking peaceful)* They are all against you, which leads me to believe you are right.

Gandhi overhears and is ready with his response.

MAHATMA GANDHI: They always first hate you and then come to the fight.

JESUS: I asked for this mission

NOSTRADAMUS: I had no idea of your first coming, but am completely confident about your second.

JESUS: I could be fooling myself, but you are right, I'm already here.

Both groups now part in synchronicity to make way for a new personage, totally unexpected.

Moses is arriving with his robe flowing in a new wind that has kicked up and is carrying his magic staff.

MOSES: Do not worship any other god, I say! I am not eloquent. My tongue is not silver and is as slow as my speech.

JESUS: Overjoyed to see you. Whatever I said new had its precedent in you.

Moses turns now directly towards Satan.

MOSES: False prophet! Your elegance and lavish garb fool only yourself.

FOOL: I am paid to be fooled.

SATAN: False possibly, but prophet nonetheless. Look around you!

He now gestures to all of these supposed sinners. Napoleon moves out of the line of sight of Satan.

NAPOLEON BONAPARTE: Don't include me. As self-proclaimed emperor, I am my own sun!

SATAN: Was it your god who helped to enslave half the world?

Before Napoleon could respond there is more commotion in the yard, now focussed on the highly animated Beethoven. We hear the chorale singing "Ode to Joy." All of the queens present have instinctively shied away from him, but Isadora is excited and turns in her dance with more fervor.

LUDWIG VON BEETHOVEN: My destiny is upon me!

He continues gesticulating as if leading an entire imaginary orchestra, but his gestures are sadly out of synch with the music. Isadora follows the music closely and intently, and now grabs Ludwig's arm to guide him into the right timing. Isadora shouts directly into his ear:

ISADORA DUNCAN: Follow me, I am "your score" in movement.

Beethoven suddenly smiles, and now follows her with his own agitated gestures.

LUDWIG VON BEETHOVEN: You saved me from myself!

Mozart looks on in awe at their performance.

WOLFGANG AMADEUS MOZART: You did it. The perfect marriage, not of Figaro, but of the opera and the symphony. I simply never had the idea.

RICHARD WAGNER: It has a nice "ring" to it.

Satan tries covering his ears, obviously in agony at the sound of Beethoven's music.

SATAN: I will get my revenge when we get to the twentieth century. You have no idea.

Einstein has been watching all this at a safe distance, but can't help overhearing Satan.

ALBERT EINSTEIN: It is now as if we are experiencing all the other centuries within this spacetime dimension.

Giordano Bruno now appears carrying a torch

GIORDANO BRUNO: What a character! I was thrown into a fire because of what I believed.

ALBERT EINSTEIN: Because of your unifying and mystical belief, right?

GIORDANO BRUNO: All the body's members are controlled by the soul living within and that soul, whole body and all the parts of the universe are vivified by a total spirit.

ALBERT EINSTEIN: They threw you in a bonfire for that.

GIORDANO BRUNO: Those were both brilliant and troubled times.

FRIEDRICH NIETZSCHE: All times are! Truth needs to arm itself against ignorance.

FOOL: I am too ignorant to know I don't know that.

Nero has not taken his eyes off that torch ever since Giordano Bruno arrived with it. Aristophanes eyes Nero and looks back nervously

ARISTOPHANES: Giordano! We should keep that torch of yours for the Greeks.

Nero now begins to stride in the direction of Giordano Bruno.

NERO: My art form is death and destruction. Whenever I see a positive light, I have an uncontrollable desire to put it out.

CALIGULA: Or "light" it up as the case may be.

Nero again pulls out his long wooden match in a threatening gesture and then tries to grab the torch from Giordano Bruno. Bruno sees what is about to happen and pulls away at the last minute from both Nero and Caligula.

GIORDANO BRUNO: That same fire that burned me cannot be turned...

Nero, with the help of Caligula, now wrestles the torch away from Giordano Bruno. Jesus sees what is happening and leaves Buddha's side to hurry over to the scuffle. He swiftly takes the torch out of Nero's hands and holds it up high.

JESUS: I am the light!

Nero shoots daggers from his eyes but Jesus is in full command of the torch. None of the others dare approach to help Nero. Beethoven starts to belt out "Ode to Joy" with fervor, still with Isadora and her dance. His hands are flying up and down imagining invisible keys he is playing parts of from his Ninth Symphony. Hildegard von Bingam joins in singing the Ninth chorus of "Ode to Joy." Both Caligula and Nero glare at Jesus in pure wrath.

NERO: Now I remember. The arena! Your crazy followers sang as they entered and were truly unafraid! How did you so empower them?

JESUS: I did nothing except to be who I am.

GEORGE BERNARD SHAW: It's a lot harder than you might imagine.

JESUS: They were able to find themselves through me.

GAUTAMA BUDDHA: Meeting your mentor!

FOOL: This is the tricky part.

WILLIAM SHAKESPEARE: You used to be exclusively mine. What happened?

FOOL: Life!...and Women! You know I wasn't always the fool, having to dig deep without a tool.

Plato shows us a look now of total contentment.

PROFESSOR PLATO: This is that exact moment in our studies where we take a step back to survey the field. We are now in the midst of a new class, yet do not know it.

Erik Satie has reappeared after being silent for so long.

ERIK SATIE: I am so foolish. I created my own religion in which I am its sole member.

A few bars of his own piano composition is heard gently in the background.

PROFESSOR PLATO: At this point we should all be learning from each other.

CARL JUNG: Some call it that point of "no return." Your commitment is so deep that it would be senseless to try to return.

FYODOR DOSTOYEVSKY: We ARE the way forward!

Another very late arrival for Plato's class is now approaching us: Francis Bacon! He is seen quickly surveying the surrounding situation.

FRANCIS BACON: Towards truth...that is so hard to tell, it sometimes needs fiction to make it plausible.

ARISTOPHANES: Well, if it isn't the "other Shakespeare" himself!

FRANCIS BACON: In reality they gave the nod to either that infamous Earl of Oxford or to Christopher Marlowe. Whoever wrote those plays obviously became his OWN mentor.

Mark Twain is still roving around here and there as the two are talking.

MARK TWAIN: So far nobody actually knows for sure, nor can prove, Shakespeare on Avon ever wrote a play in his life.

Johann Kepler has been circling around the area till he finally decides to enter where the two groups have now gathered.

JOHANN KEPLER: These arguments are too circular for my taste. Elliptical thinking is exactly what is needed to express and understand a deeper truth. The orbits of the planets are ALSO elliptical, not circular as was once believed.

FRANCIS BACON: So true, Mr. Kepler. Some books are to be tasted, others to be swallowed, but mine are among the few to be slowly chewed for digestion.

Gurdjieff has also returned after having left for a while, observing the behavior of the gang of outsiders. He looks at Francis Bacon as he is speaking.

G.I. GURDJIEFF: Now here's a man who has dug a hole or two.

FRANCIS BACON: Do you want to say that each one is his own mentor?

G.I. GURDJIEFF: Close, but not exactly. You need a teacher and need to know when it is time for you to show what you know

SOCRATES: Or not know...

LAO-TZU: Enemies can help too, so long as you truly know them.

There is more commotion on the side of our agitators, especially with Nero and Caligula. Nero shouts out in a high brazen voice.

NERO: As Shakespeare has reminded us: until now, all is prologue.

FOOL: Say what you mean! Don't be a fool!

NERO: I have been misleading everyone by playing the part of "Nero." That is clearly not who I am, nor ever was.

FOOL: You fool! You just can't do that! We are all making history here, and you're trying to turn it into a comedy.

Herodotus arrives, having been invited by Plato originally to document and write about his classes at this school of Ancient Learning. Plato always referred to him as the "Father of History."

HERODOTUS: Who here is trying to say that history is a comedy?

The fool points clearly to Nero who has gone strangely quiet.

HERODOTUS: Here Mister, trying to change your story, rewrite history?

Francis Bacon has brought his new book entitled: "New Atlantis," which he had planned to show to Plato and his class members.

NERO: I am more familiar with your book, Sir Francis, than I am with you. Whether you wrote those Shakespeare plays or not has far less interest for me than your ideas on "utopia."

Nero has clearly gotten Bacon's attention now, as he continues on.

NERO: I never wanted to burn anything down, least of all my beloved Rome. My utopian "Golden House" I constructed, might have been a good illustration of what you always wanted to do!

FOOL: The only true utopia comes from the mind of a wise man. Yet the catch is, if he is wise he will maintain the position as "the fool."

FRANCIS BACON: In my "utopia" there is a house for the school "Solomon's House."

FOOL: I have still not graduated from the "School for Fools."

DANTE ALIGHIERI: For some weird reason I seem to get both you, Francis Bacon, and Nero. Are both of you familiar with the third part of my "Divine Comedy?"

FRANCIS BACON: Yes, please go on, Señor Dante!

DANTE ALIGHIERI: I depict my "Paradise" as a series of concentric spheres that surround the Earth consisting of the Moon, Mercury, Venus, the Sun, Mars, Jupiter, Saturn, the Fixed Stars and the Primum Mobile.

FRANCIS BACON: Don't try to sugar-coat the journey, Dante.

JESUS: Your book, Dante, represents the soul's ascent to Heaven.

GAUTAMA BUDDHA: There is just that last circle of fire that exists in Earth's "upper atmosphere."

FRANCIS BACON: I know your "Paradise," Dante, and its nine Celestial Spheres of Heaven.

JOHANN KEPLER: If you had known, Dante, wouldn't you have meant to say that your nine spheres are not concentric but elliptical?

DANTE ALIGHIERI: Of course, but it's more important symbolically rather than factually. We all know that, Mr. Kepler.

JESUS: I will meet you all in Paradise as your Mentor!

JOHANN KEPLER: The sound that all these spheres produce through their movement I have called: "The Harmony of the Spheres!"

III

From Classroom to Courtyard and Back

Plato looks around his classroom to see who has returned to class and who has remained out in the schoolyard.

PROFESSOR PLATO: I am beginning to rethink my "Republic"!

ARISTOPHANES: *(Asking Plato with his usual touch of irony)* How so?

PROFESSOR PLATO: It is now time for a new approach. I could have been wrong about a few things.

GEORGE BERNARD SHAW: You mean that our life is not about finding yourself in any particular school system but...

FRIEDRICH NIETZSCHE: ...but what?

GEORGE BERNARD SHAW: ...about creating yourself. Take science for example. It never solved a problem without creating ten more.

PROFESSOR PLATO: I am remembering again my cave allegory.

WILLIAM SHAKESPEARE: Be brief Master, otherwise you betray the soul of wit.

ARISTOPHANES: If there is no humor, you will lose half your audience!

PROFESSOR PLATO: The cave is important because…

The sudden loud noise of two voices from the yard drowns out Plato's voice.

MACHIAVELLI: We are in the midst of a crisis in leadership. All around us I see enormous talent of visionaries and creative geniuses, but who will come forward to actually lead?

Jesus had chosen not to go back into the classroom just yet to stay outside with the group of troublemakers.

JESUS: It is written, and I have been told it will be me.

Both Hemingway and Fitzgerald never did make it into the class.

ERNEST HEMINGWAY: Maybe so, yet I do not believe it. I have written myself out and off. That "blank page" has me beat at the moment.

F. SCOTT FITZGERALD: But you had quite a run at it "Papa!"

ERNEST HEMINGWAY: Yes, but I fell short of my mark.

In the middle of their dialog, we hear more loud noises of hammering from some kind of serious construction going on in another part of the yard outside, which until now no one had paid much attention to. Picasso is over there near the construction site with his shirt off and madly painting and creating sculptures.

PABLO PICASSO: Looks like there is a large ship under construction.

The main builder now looks up realizing that he is being scrutinized. It is, of course, none other than Noah.

NOAH: This is not a cave that I have heard so much about coming from Plato's lips, but a complete nave that not only floats but will become queen of all ships.

SOLOMON: We are both connected through "Our Ark."

JESUS: Both of your "arks" refer to Salvation from Waters.

ALEXANDER PUSHKIN: We still have your "Ark," Solomon, under our protection in Ethiopia...

MOSES: ...Containing my commandments written on those stone tablets.

Moses is seen wielding his staff, as imposing as ever. In the distance we hear the sound of trumpets being blown. King David appears for the first time bearing his iconic slingshot. Appearing as suddenly as Noah, we now have a renewed hope of some kind of salvation.

Michelangelo, who also did not go back inside for Plato's class, is there near Picasso and the construction site.

MICHELANGELO: You look quite different in real life from how I pictured you in my sculpture.

KING DAVID: You failed to capture fully my three sides: warrior, poet and musician.

KING SOLOMON: Your Book of Psalms saved me in dire moments as King and further inspired me to write my "Songs." Your "Psalms" are instrumental music in the shape of words.

MICHELANGELO: I guess I might have chipped too much of that marble stone away.

PABLO PICASSO: Or not enough.

WILLIAM SHAKESPEARE: Striving to better we oft mar what was good.

FOOL: This is the "real school" not for a fool.

KING DAVID: We need a leader who is a choirmaster.

Beethoven is ranting while imagining that his orchestra is still playing with him directing the musicians. He intinctively feels he has been called again for something.

LUDWIG VON BEETHOVEN: Choose me as your orchestra leader. Being nearly totally deaf, I am also the ideal husband according to Michel Montaigne.

Beethoven points to him as he is just now entering the class.

MICHEL MONTAIGNE: I quote others only in order to better express myself.

ISADORA DUNCAN: Women of the world take note. Here is your ideal man, full of music to make your heart dance, yet cannot hear a note of it.

FOOL: Plus, he can't hear any of your complaints. Perfect!

Plato is noting that not everyone has come back to class.

CARL JUNG: What were you just saying about your cave allegory?

PROFESSOR PLATO: Never mind. I don't have all your attention anymore anyway. Most of you are mesmerized by the drama unfolding out there in the schoolyard.

Outside, there is now a group of observers around Noah, having come from both sides of the playground yard.

NOAH: I have never stopped shipbuilding.

KING SOLOMON: As I said, our two "arks" complement one another.

JESUS: Those "waters" are all inside of us.

Moses now raises up his magical staff.

MOSES: To rise like this! *(He raises the Staff with his voice.)* If I can make those waters part, you can surely make them rise up practicing your art.

Mark Twain starts laughing once again.

MARK TWAIN: Often it does seem such a pity that Noah and his party did not miss the boat!

FOOL: There is a man after my own heart.

NOSTRADAMUS: Those who got saved ultimately could not save themselves.

CARL JUNG: All so symbolic.

WILLIAM BLAKE: I have illustrated all this through my watercolor visions.

JESUS: The true Ark of God is the human body!

WILLIAM BLAKE: Exactly!

JESUS: It is not a temple made with hands, but the hands ARE the Temple.

WILLIAM BLAKE: The "flood" is of the Imagination!

KING SOLOMON: Then we have found our new leader!

FRIEDRICH NIETZSCHE: Who is?

KING DAVID: Not who, but what?

WILLIAM BLAKE: The Imagination! We are its followers.

PROFESSOR PLATO: Wow!! This approach blows my "Republic" right out of those "waters." Maybe I am done as "Instructor" and must give way to "Constructor."

FOOL: This new "school of the fool" is its own teaching tool.

WILLIAM BLAKE: Let the cherubs now sing!

KING SOLOMON: Amen!

King David takes out his harp, puts down his slingshot and begins to play. As he plays we see that our group of women have been quiet for a while as they listen intently to the music of the harp.

ISADORA DUNCAN: *(She continues to whirl in her diaphanous Greek gown.)* How can anyone resist those soothing tones?

Mozart, unable to resist, picks up one his least favorite instruments, the flute, and begins to play an infectious melody. Salome uses her "head" well and dances together with Isadora.

SALOME: John, I did you wrong. Please return in spirit to baptize me in these waters that rise within.

NOAH: My Ark is ready in this flood of emotion to embark. Who will join me?

Not everyone there in the yard at the "school" was in the same uptempo mood. More rumblings began "flooding" from those troubled outsiders.

KARL MARX: That Ark is not for the people. It is only being built with a crew to save an elite few.

CHARLES DARWIN: You won't survive if you are not fit for it, Herr Marx. How have you actually struggled personally while you preach this "class struggle"?

Marx grumbles something and waves Darwin away. Plato has literally given up with his "struggle" to create a "class structure" inside and returns to the yard where most of his "students" have remained anyway.

PROFESSOR PLATO: The struggle for "class" is more important than this "class struggle."

ISADORA DUNCAN: I just say yes to Grecian classical art!

She whirls and whirls, mimicking the designs on those ancient Grecian vases which originally inspired her to create the "new" dance barefoot. In the meantime, Leonardo has been finishing his sketch of Nefertiti. As he puts on the final touches, Casanova, who had not been around nor been invited by Plato, strangely appears and is immediately attracted to Nefertiti. She, on the other hand, is not impressed with his advances.

NEFERTITI: Even if you know 101 ways to make love, where is your girlfriend?

CASANOVA: I do not conquer, I submit!

Nefertiti turns away from him to showcase her immortal profile for Leonardo to finish his portrait.

NEFERTITI: I want to be conquered...with kindness!

CASANOVA: My art is to tread on the brink of the precipice without falling in.

NEFERTITI: We train with balancing and stretching exercises to maintain nimble minds.

CASANOVA: I have changed my ways. Let me tell you how. Come walk with me!

Nefertiti and Casanova go off together as Mary now approaches.

LEONARD DAVINCI: Does everyone want to paint you or is it more just me?

MARY: You have already done me with my child in my arms.

LEONARD DAVINCI: I know, now I need you childless.

Mary tentatively agrees for Leonardo to have another go at her portrait, this time without Jesus.

MARY: I have always been told I make a good model.

Back to Casanova and Nefertiti strolling around the yard.

CASANOVA: The sweetest pleasures are those which are the hardest to be won.

Their voices fade as they move away.

PROFESSOR PLATO: Listen, this is the beginning phase of a university. Socrates was once my teacher and you, Aristotle, can vouch for me as your teacher.

ARISTOTLE: The question has always been who is the expert and who is the searcher.

PROFESSOR PLATO: Knowledge comes from your questioning, not from my teaching.

ARISTOTLE: You have always lobbied for the continuation of the arts along with philosophy and writing.

Plato looks around the yard to try and decide how to move forward with the class. It appeared as if their period of "classroom experience" had ended and that from now on they would all continue to interact outside in the schoolyard. Gurdjieff still carries his shovel in his hand and now brandishes it once more high up in the air.

G.I. GURDJIEFF: Only through discipline can you awaken. We are all merely sheep, still very fast asleep.

WILLIAM SHAKESPEARE: We are such stuff as dreams are made of, and our little life is rounded with a sleep.

FOOL: Just awaken to a "light" kiss.

WILLIAM SHAKESPEARE: Sleep knits that raveled sleeve of care.

Leonardo puts down the brush of the painting "Mary without Child."

LEONARD DAVINCI: I love a twenty-minute nap every four hours.

Mozart is bounding around always looking like he is memorizing a score or looking through his own imagination for more.

WOLFGANG AMADEUS MOZART: My composing "muse" keeps me up till around 1 a.m., then I sleep till 6 and continue composing throughout the morning.

SIGMUND FREUD: Because of all my self-medicating I must get in six hours per night.

VOLTAIRE: Thanks to Bach, who turned me on to coffee, I drink around forty cups a day and just barely still get my four hours of sleep.

WINSTON CHURCHILL: My naps are the keys to my success. I always have kept a bed in the House of Parliament.

FOOL: I am too foolish to ever know what time it is. I am always mistaking the sun for the moon and vice versa.

HIPPOCRATES: Sleep is the best medicine!

MICHEL MONTAIGNE: Actually, Dr. Hippocrates, we are the sleeping awake and the awake sleeping.

Picasso has been roving around back and forth across the schoolyard and now has found a bicycle seat and handlebars. He lifts up the handlebars in front of his face for all to see while holding the bicycle seat underneath them.

PABLO PICASSO: What do you think of my idea for a "bull sculpture" made from these bicycle parts, Vincent? Once you have mastered those rules of creating like a pro, you can then go ahead and break them like an artist.

The Fool immediately notices the bull made from two bicycle parts and comments.

FOOL: Trapped in the duality of the bicycle.

Plato intervenes here to rant again about artists.

PROFESSOR PLATO: Artists! Artists! Troublemakers. Leave Vincent be!

Back inside the classroom, a huge clock on the wall starts to melt. Back outside, Einstein is deep in thought.

ALBERT EINSTEIN: The clock is the only place in our western civilization that unifies time and space!

The scene is now set for the belated, yet grand, entrance of Salvador Dali. He is riding a white horse with his wife, Gala, on the same horse with both legs to one side, naked, like Lady Godiva. Her long flowing hair covers part of her naked body.

SALVADOR DALI: I brought my Muse in flesh and blood to our celebration.

Now with the "torch" handed to Aristophanes from Jesus, Aristophanes returns to centerstage.

ARISTOPHANES: Of the "School of Dialog" or as some say, both the academies of learning and unlearning…

Dali with his free hand raises a glass of red wine in an oversize goblet.

SALVADOR DALI: A real wine requires a mad man to grow the vine, a wise man to tend it, a poet to make it and a lover to drink it!

Michelangelo looks over only mildly amused and gets back to his search for the ideal marble.

MICHELANGELO: My "David" is just around the corner.

Picasso is listening and looks over at him working with the marble.

PABLO PICASSO: You know, Señor, when I was a kid I drew like you draw, but it took me the rest of my life to draw like a kid.

MICHELANGELO: *(Scoffing)* A simple case of having nowhere to go but down.

Dali, totally on his own trip and causing a sensation with his Muse, Gala, is still holding the goblet high.

SALVADOR DALI: I do not take drugs! I AM drugs!

William Blake is excited by this highly charged atmosphere.

WILLIAM BLAKE: I am a visionary, but not from ingesting mushrooms. Your "head" IS the mushroom!

SALVADOR DALI: I cannot believe you were not Spanish or even French. How did you manage?

WILLIAM BLAKE: It was not easy dealing with Joshua's pursuit of general truth and beauty through his "fashionable" oil portraits.

Joshua Reynolds is in the background, a long-term enemy of Blake and also a highly successful portrait painter.

JOSHUA REYNOLDS: I became the Royal Academy's first president and...

WILLIAM BLAKE: To generalize as you do is to be an idiot.

JOSHUA REYNOLDS: You are a hypocrite not courageous enough to put your ideals into practice.

WILLIAM BLAKE: My Imagination embraces the "Body of God." The Vision presents itself to me as its handmaiden.

Jesus is loving this duel and of course sides with Blake.

JESUS: It is a pity you could not finish your brilliant depiction of those biblical scenes and settings. You "saw" the Light!

Dali steals the stage once again…

SALVADOR DALI: In fact, I myself do not understand what my painting means—while painting them does not imply that they are meaningless.

FOOL: *(Laughing)* It has been said the symbol precedes its illumination!

WILLIAM SHAKESPEARE: Finally, you say something not stolen from me.

Gauguin is standing near Van Gogh, nervous about what he'll do next.

PAUL GAUGUIN: I shut my eyes in order to see.

VINCENT VAN GOGH: I open mine to see where I am going.

LEONARD DA VINCI: I awoke only to see the rest of the world still asleep.

MICHELANGELO: So you are the only "awakened one?"

A North American teepee has been put up in the schoolyard. At this very moment "Black Elk" emerges to steal some of the show from Dali.

BLACK ELK: The life of the Native American is like the wings of the air. Sometimes dreams are wiser than waking. When pure power comes through me I am able to cure.

Dali stops his white horse in front of Black Elk's teepee still carrying Gala.

SALVADOR DALI: I've always wanted to meet a real live "Medicine Man." I have heard so much about your powerful bows and visions of rainbows.

Black Elk looks up at the sky, seeing a large thunderbolt in formation.

BLACK ELK: When I breathe, my breath is lightning.

As Black Elk pronounces the word, lightning strikes nearby where the Hitler crowd gathered. Black Elk begins to sing as his wife emerges from the teepee to join in inspiring him to pick up his Native American flute to play. Dali looks inquisitively at a large "sand painting" on one side of the teepee and a "healing rug" on the other.

SALVADOR DALI: This is a whole other "trip," Gala. Let's check it out.

Black Elk motions to Dali and Gala to enter the "paintings" to absorb their energy. They each go to stand in one, Dali in the middle of the sand painting and Gala in the middle of the magically woven rug.

SALVADOR DALI : This may be one of those days when I "die" of an overdose of satisfaction.

GALA: You and me both. It is like getting married for the third time.

They reach out to hold each other's hands. Hippocrates has drifted over to where the teepee is located and is fascinated by the scene.

HIPPOCRATES: I have said walking is the best medicine, but what I am witnessing should rank way up there, too. This is incredible stuff.

Black Elk stops playing his flute and looks at Hippocrates in his Greek toga.

BLACK ELK: I feel that we might be "brothers-of-the-cure."

HIPPOCRATES: I, too, am a servant and facilitator of Nature. I believe the natural forces within us are the true healers.

Black Elk shows his hands upward to the open sky and points to the four directions with his flute.

BLACK ELK: A frog does not drink up the pond in which he lives...

Plato now has completely lost control over the class and that classroom experience. He tried unsuccessfully to get them back in after their "recess" to no avail. Who knows what will happen from now on? This is without doubt the "The Great Deal." He is in the yard with his special toga of the teacher flapping in the wind of the storm Black elk had created with his chanting and music.

PROFESSOR PLATO: I have to review my lesson plan that was once mapped out when I taught you, Aristotle. Do you remember any of it?

ARISTOTLE: I do, headmaster, but don't know how we can apply it from here on out. Everything appears to have changed.

PROFESSOR PLATO: It seems as though I have become a cave.

ARISTOPHANES: The classroom was your "cave" where you mistook the "shadows" of pupils coming and going for their complete true beings.

PROFESSOR PLATO: And now here in the school's yard...?

ARISTOPHANES: They are who they are, as you are, too!

Satan senses the disarray of the school system and secretly rejoices. It is written all over his face. Samuel Becket, always watching and never participating, is now nearby.

SAMUEL BECKET: I am NOT the one I have been waiting for.

FOOL: Of course you are, you fool! What more did you expect?

SAMUEL BECKET: I just waited too long to act out my dream!

FOOL: But you are not alone in your analysis that led to your paralysis.

SATAN: I admire you, Becket, for being above it all by choosing to do nothing. Your hands are still "clean."

Leonardo has wandered in his curiosity to the other side, where Hitler's gang is still grouped together, and now speaks directly to Satan.

LEONARD DA VINCI: Life is pretty simple: You do stuff. Most fail. Some work. You do more of what works.

Satan looks at Leonardo up and down and scoffs disapprovingly.

SATAN: You are what they have called: "A Renaissance Man."

LEONARD DA VINCI: YOU are calling me that! I am open-minded and do what I can.

Satan opens and closes his black cape with its red, velvet lining. Leonardo moves on, apparently not impressed with him.

PABLO PICASSO: You, more than most music and art, are a guiding light.

Picasso glares at both Satan and Becket.

SAMUEL BECKET: Waiting for that "right moment" in order to act.

PABLO PICASSO: That moment is right now! It never seems right, that's why it is—you make it right!

SAMUEL BECKET: None of this computes.

PABLO PICASSO: Computers are useless. They can only give you answers.

Dali is feeling amazing from that positive energy of "standing" in the Native American sand painting.

SALVADOR DALI: Gala and I are on a quest. Believe it or not.

Black Elk is back playing the Native American flute. In the meantime Karl Marx is still playing around with the gang and is laughing.

KARL MARX: I call this the "class struggle."

SIGMUND FREUD: You always said it was about class.

WOLFGANG AMADEUS MOZART: Though not the least bit "classy."

Beethoven is still being guided around by Isadora Duncan.

LUDWIG VON BEETHOVEN: Class?! Did I hear that word? What class? Where?

Isadora now yells into his ear.

ISADORA DUNCAN: YOU are my class act, Ludwig. You hear with your soul, not your ears!

LUDWIG VON BEETHOVEN: After deafness set in I chose to go on because of my Art. I still had something to give.

ISADORA DUNCAN: And give you did. I listen to your Fifth Symphony every day just to jump start my dancing art.

RICHARD WAGNER: Who knows what direction music will take after me. We are at a watershed.

Black Elk puts down his flute and there is silence.

SATAN: You will see something like never before! And enjoy these last moments...

JESUS: What trickery! You will hide all your devious actions under the guise of "progress."

GAUTAMA BUDDHA: Then, who could argue?

Nijinsky has not gone off anywhere, but has one of his drawings in his hand and is muttering in a loud voice!

VASLAV NIJINSKY: Now I will dance you the war...the war you did not prevent.

Nijinsky still dressed as a "faun," an animal spirit, dances freely everywhere in the yard in a different style than Isadora with many more "modern" movements. As things become more chaotic and comedic with the arrival of Dali, Gala and Black Elk, Moliere arrives, now at last.

MOLIERE: I see that the real duty of comedy is to correct men by amusing them!

Nijinsky and Isadora briefly interact in the center of the yard, each still continuing with their own style of dance.

MOLIERE: All the ills of mankind, all the tragic misfortunes that fill history books, all the political blunders, all the failures of the great leaders...

Moliere points to all the different "leaders" there in the yard outside of Plato's classroom.

MOLIERE: ...have arisen from a lack of dancing!

Rimbaud is around, still appearing slightly drunk, but attempting to take in all that is going on.

ARTHUR RIMBAUD: Misfortune was my god, but genius is able to recover my childhood at will.

MOLIERE: I live on good soup, not on the finery of words.

Becket is, of course, still on the sidelines and waiting.

SAMUEL BECKET: Words are all we have!

More rumbling on the gang's side as Hitler begins a tirade.

ADOLF HITLER: Though a leader, I am not Napoleon, a dealer of hope. It is good fortune for governments that people do not think.

NAPOLEON BONAPARTE: I also deal in religion, the only way we can protect ourselves from the poor.

ADOLF HITLER: Just focus on being victorious and, trust me, in the end you will never be asked if you told the truth.

MAO ZEDONG: Make sure you use a long stick if you plan on waking the tiger.

GENGHIS KHAN: Why do you worry? You, yourself, said they were made of paper.

Plato looks over to Aristophanes, worried.

PROFESSOR PLATO: We are quickly losing out grip, our hold over them.

ARISTOPHANES: Then just release your grip to be able to better enjoy the trip.

This word "trip" begins to mysteriously reverberate throughout the yard as a new arrival is noticed by Blake. This newcomer, Aldous Huxley, is conservatively dressed in comparison with the flamboyance of Satan's red velvet cape lining.

WILLIAM BLAKE: If our doors of perception were cleansed, everything would appear to us as infinite.

ALDOUS HUXLEY: Beauty is worse than wine, it intoxicates both the holder AND the beholder.

WILLIAM BLAKE: You have seen my watercolor visions?

ALDOUS HUXLEY: Yes, but I had to use mescaline to get there.

WILLIAM BLAKE: My drug, as well as my god, is the Imagination! I worship its wings that navigate what it brings.

ALDOUS HUXLEY: You are the only writer/artist I knew who successfully used both as your artistic crew.

Eve reappears again looking now so other-worldly and exhibiting a strange inner glow.

EVE: You remember I am "Eve," as a new morning followed my last evening.

Huxley is clearly taken away and gasps remembering that he is stone sober, but is he dreaming?

ALDOUS HUXLEY: "The" Eve!"

Blake is smiling broadly now and loving every moment.

WILLIAM BLAKE: Just as I pictured you in my watercolor painting.

EVE: You mean when you heard those words: "and she shall be called woman?"

ALDOUS HUXLEY: I loved that watercolor from your Biblical illustrations.

WILLIAM BLAKE: I simply called it: "Creation of Eve."

EVE: You are probably wondering about Adam.

ALDOUS HUXLEY: Yes!

WILLIAM BLAKE: I once "saw" him as a hermaphrodite, but never could capture that in a watercolor piece.

EVE: Because he is many, an entire race, that inspired all that has manifested.

ALDOUS HUXLEY: There are things known and there are things unknown...and in between are the "doors of perception."

WILLIAM BLAKE: That can only be opened after cleansed by the Imagination!

PROFESSOR PLATO: I, too, am familiar with that androgyne race of Adam. It was before the sexes divided into two. Then knowledge was absolute. Each one *was* a Tree of Knowledge!

ARISTOTLE: Its branches bearing fruit became my life long pursuit.

FOOL: I was the one who tricked everyone regarding this tree saying that the fruit was forbidden.

PROFESSOR PLATO: We have been forever in search of our Other Half after this split!

CARL JUNG: This is my "anima."

SIGMUND FREUD: Your what?

CARL JUNG: Each male has an inner creative female and each female an inner male.

GAUTAMA BUDDHA: It is the classic "yin-yang" symbol in western terminology.

ARISTOTLE: Happiness still depends only on ourselves.

EVE: I am a reminder, a finder.

ALDOUS HUXLEY: Of what?

EVE: Of your own "door of perception." Through it you access the beyond.

Aristophanes points up into the air at an imaginary spot up ahead.

ARISTOPHANES: Following the road of the "Adams," there is the stone and the steps.

Peter is now there at the side of Jesus looking on with intent at all that is happening.

JESUS: Peter, you are that "cornerstone" upon which all will be built.

PETER: As a fisherman on the high seas, I knew that the boat was stronger than I.

JESUS: Now you *are* that boat to carry others who know not how to
"float."

PETER: Eve! Do you mind if I use Nefertitti's profile model to carve our "bowhead?"

EVE: She is one of my incarnations among all the nations.

PROFESSOR PLATO: I believe I once wrote about all this. We are leaving that "Inner Cave" and its shadows to which we have been for so long its slave.

ARISTOTLE: Where are all of our explorers, unmatched, who have already been dispatched?

PROFESSOR PLATO: Who do you mean?

ARISTOTLE: Christopher Columbus, David Livingstone and Daniel Boone, for starters.

Their conversation is interrupted with new commotion. Entering the schoolyard now is King David.

KING DAVID: Where is Saul so I can cure him of his nightmares and give you're a gift?

More yelling from the gang's side of the yard. Hitler is looking up at this extremely tall stranger.

ADOLF HITLER: Don't much care what you call yourself, but I could really use a giant like you.

This is that same storm that arose when Black Elk spoke to the clouds. Now the next bolt comes which Goliath is able to reach out and grab. He now stands firm, his head almost in that cloud formed by Black Elk.

KING DAVID: Saul! The head you so coveted will soon be safely here within these Jerusalem walls.

David now spots Goliath again and this time reaches for his sling and stone.

Jesus suddenly sees the potential for a violent outbreak.

JESUS: David, my King, you have no need to prove yourself, once again, the warrior you already are.

Dali is still totally relaxed and apparently in a privileged state after being in Black Elk's sand painting, but gazes out at what is unfolding before him.

SALVADOR DALI: Even I could not have come up with what we are about to see.

Goliath looks down at Hitler like an annoying fly and tries to just swat him away. Hitler attempts to dodge the swing. Goliath is still dressed in his full armor.

GOLIATH: Who has seen my javelin?

David yells out challengingly.

KING DAVID: It is that spear you believe we all fear!

Goliath explodes in wrath, grabs his javelin that he has suddenly located, and hurls it in the direction of King David. Jesus, in desperation, booms out for all.

JESUS: Blessed are the peacemakers for they...

The javelin strikes the ground just at the feet of King David. Saul is standing right next to where the javelin has struck.

SAUL: The crown is now yours, King David.

KING DAVID: But where is my kingdom? Here battling the giant Goliath one more time?

In the background we now hear guitar strumming in the style of John Dowland.

SAUL: I would be a liar if I did not say that is the music of a lyre.

KING DAVID: Of course I know it—my soul is a poet.

GOLIATH: But YOU are here! This field is not for study, but for battle.

JESUS: I, too, have come to bring the "sword"...to cut down untruth!

Dali is still in heaven from his stay in the center of that medicinal sand painting. He grabs and raises a huge paint brush that has been transformed from that javelin, which moments before had left the massive hands of Goliath. It was transformed by the magical touch of Dali, empowered by the Medicine Man, Black Elk.

BLACK ELK: Now you can see how this "medicine" works. It takes YOU at that same moment you take it.

FOOL: This is the "mediscene!"

WILLIAM SHAKESPEARE: You have all been waiting for.

SAMUEL BECKET: Why don't I feel like the wait is over?

King David picks up his lyre and puts down his slingshot to play. As Goliath visibly starts to calm down against his own wishes, we witness his struggle.

Joan of Arc's horse calms and is also mesmerized by the sound of the lyre. Plato now has a contented look for the very first time. He motions to the gang on the side of Goliath, visibly unhappy with this sudden peaceful turn of events. Julius Caesar has now come to his side.

JULIUS CAESAR: My empire began to contract when it could not expand any more.

ALBERT EINSTEIN: Just like the galaxies in the universe.

FOOL: Didn't someone worth remembering once say: "As above, so below?"

WILLIAM SHAKESPEARE: It is not in the stars to hold our destiny, but in ourselves.

Henry Miller has quietly just arrived from his long stay in Paris and is surveying the situation in a very detached manner.

HENRY MILLER: Every man has his own destiny: the only imperative is to follow it, to accept it, no matter where it leads him.

Miller glances over at Jesus and Aristophanes. Aristophanes has already handed the "torch" back to Jesus.

JESUS: This burning torch given to me by Aristophanes is now inside me and can never be taken away.

Heraclitus, also a very late arrival, is now present for Plato's class, which has yet to get reorganized after their long recess.

HERACLITUS: Sorry for my late arrival. I have been trying to enter that same stream twice. *(He laughs at himself.)*

FOOL: To discover what, you fool!

HERACLITUS: That I could not do it.

FOOL: I don't need a stream to help me follow my dream.

SOCRATES: I still know nothing, and yet they still killed me for that.

FOOL: Imagine if you had known something like our Head of the School here.

SOCRATES: You referring to my student Plato?

FOOL: Yes, that guy over there that is running this "school for the fool." In other words, in my honor.

SOCRATES: How did you escape?

FOOL: It was the only wise decision I ever made. I had the backing of you, buddy, on that one.

He looks over at Aristophanes.

SOCRATES: Buddy?

FOOL: I am smarter than I think I am, but not as smart as I would like to be.

Aristophanes hears his name come up and responds.

ARISTOPHANES: I am not as smart as I think I am, but smarter than I would like to be.

HERACLITUS: Character is destiny!

William James is another late arrival who is also trying to understand what is going on in the School.

WILLIAM JAMES: And to get there we need a great weapon to do battle with the stress of the journey.

FOOL: Any bright ideas?

WILLIAM JAMES: It is our ability to choose one thought over another.

The new smoke is now arising has nothing to do with that earlier fire play between Nero and Caligula. It is coming from the mouth of a newcomer in the yard, Groucho Marx and the cigar he is smoking.

GROUCHO MARX: Has anyone seen my brother, Karl, I got word that he is here?

FOOL: No one mentioned anything about you two being brothers.

GROUCHO MARX: Me neither…if not for my mother—tongue.

Karl Marx seeing the cloud of cigar smoke arising and holds up his recently written "Manifesto."

KARL MARX: Are you that other Marx I heard about, a time-waster and nothing more? At least I am trying to make the world a better place.

GROUCHO MARX: From the very moment I picked up your book, Karl, until I laid it down, I was convulsed with laughter. Someday I intend to read it.

FOOL: They call ME crazy. At least now I am not feeling so alone.

Groucho Marx looks over at Karl and examines his cohorts.

GROUCHO MARX: I've had a perfectly wonderful evening, but this wasn't it.

Black Elk looks on fascinated by all that smoke coming out of Groucho's cigar. He walks over to him.

BLACK ELK: Here, try this pipe. We all share our smoke. It is the best medicine.

But before Groucho can accept this peace pipe, his brother Harpo arrives playing a small portable harp. King David immediately notices the other harp player now next to Groucho.

KING DAVID: Who are you?

Harpo says nothing but shrugs his shoulders, points to Groucho and continues playing his small harp.

KING DAVID: Brothers?

GROUCHO MARX: This is my surreal brother.

KING DAVID: *(Obviously on unfamiliar ground)* What do you mean?

Dali comes back to earth hearing the world "surreal."

SALVADOR DALI: Surreal? Did someone just call? Where is my canvas? I need to paint now, immediately or die.

He holds up that gigantic brush that he had "magically" transformed from Goliath's thrown javelin. With brush in hand he returns to the sand painting. The music of the lyre continues being played by King David together now with Harpo's small harp. Isadora leaves Beethoven's side to resume her dance of Grecian turns. Just back from Egypt, William Butler Yeats has joined this motley crowd.

WILLIAM BUTLER YEATS: How can I know the dancer from the dance?

Black Elk had picked up his Native American flute to play again as Rumi, who has also just arrived form the Middle East, starts to whirl together with Isadora in a dervish style.

RUMI: You shouldn't be able to know. One is the other and the other becomes One.

ISADORA DUNCAN: This has always been my dream to whirl like a planet.

Leonardo looks up from his painting of Nefertiti to comment.

LEONARD DA VINCI: Simplicity is the ultimate sophistication.

Karl Marx slowly inches his way across the schoolyard with his "Manifesto" clutched in his hand.

KARL MARX: How could we be brothers?

ADOLF HITLER: Yeah, exactly my thoughts.

Rumi is still whirling to the flute of Black Elk.

RUMI: Let the beauty of what you love be what you do!

FOOL: Nothing foolish about that advice. It's only "vice" is to be overly virtuous.

Stalin had been overly quiet for too long and now has had enough of all this music and dancing. He stands up and speaks in a booming voice.

JOSEPH STALIN: Didn't I read somewhere when I was a young student at St Petersburg that you, "Professor" Plato wanted no artists in your ideal Republic?

VLADMIR LENIN: I read that too! Any "cook" should be able to run his imaginary "Republic."

JOSEPH STALIN: Of course, the cook just needs to know when to increase the heat and add salt.

VLADIMIR LENIN: But not so much unless you are putting it on wounds!

Both laugh gregariously, as we hear over their laughter the clear sound of a gigantic gong announcing the reappearance of Genghis Kahn. He is seated on a horse as pure black as his helmet.

GENGHIS KHAN: Remember you have no companions but your own shadow. What is all that noise I am hearing in the yard?

JOSEPH STALIN: The artists here are having their fun now in the sun.

Genghis Kahn looks over at Dali with both disgust and disdain.

GENGHIS KHAN: How can one do battle brandishing a mere paint brush?

Lao-Tzu interrupts his long period of deep meditation to respond.

LAO-TZU: In the twentieth way to write the word "sword," the calligrapher's swordplay technique is revealed.

Genghis Kahn glances over at this wandering philosopher in his Chinese garb.

GENGHIS KHAN: I believe I once flowed through your land like water through a sieve.

LAO-TZU: Yes, and in your ignorance forgot about our dangerous school of calligraphy.

Rumi overhears their conversation and decides to chime in.

RUMI: I once encountered one of these "artists" during my travels. His swordplay was purely art, just as the dance can guise a lethal move of the fighter.

Lenin, off to the side, is not happy with this idle banter in his view.

VLADMIR LENIN: Sometimes history needs a little push.

Goliath is now awakening from the bewitching music of Black Elk, Harpo and King David.

GOLIATH: And I am that giant available to carry out whatever is necessary.

ADOLF HITLER: We could all use that "final push."

RUMI: The wound is exactly that place where the light enters.

VLADIMIR LENIN: You must have gone astray from Plato's Academy!

JOSEPH STALIN: All his whirling has already made me dizzy. That is definitely something our "new schools" will not be offering.

Goliath stands with his feet in a wide stance and stares down at Stalin who gazes up at him.

GOLIATH: What?!

JOSEPH STALIN: How tall?

GOLIATH: Six cubits and a span.

Goliath had long since relinquished those two lightning bolts he had grabbed during Black Elk's rain dance that had provoked the thunderstorm.

ADOLF HITLER: What beast could carry him?

HANNIBAL: Possibly one of my elephants. I have one large one particularly in mind.

GENGHIS KHAN: Let's get on with the battle. If you are afraid, don't do it. If you're doing it don't be afraid.

There are many battles to fight and rewards to go to the victors but what of the discoverers and their adventurous plight? Vasco da Gama enters the yard now brimming with confidence to set sail.

VASCO DA GAMA: I am not afraid of darkness. Real death is preferable to a life without living.

Christopher Columbus has also entered, following Da Gama to stand in the middle of the yard. He quietly surveys the two groups.

CHRISTOPHER COLUMBUS: We need to follow the light of the sun if we are to leave this old world.

Nicolaus Copernicus swaggers on in as the sun pokes out around one of Black Elk's leftover thunderclouds.

NICOLAUS COPERNICUS: Finally, we shall place the Sun himself at the center of the Universe.

Johannes Kepler has been circling around the yard for the last hour and now moves to its center where Copernicus is standing.

NICOLAUS COPERNICUS: Great to see you again, Kepler. I remember well that Chianti we had in Venice together.

JOHANNES KEPLER: You were such a long way from Poland. Wasn't it just after your book was banned?

NICOLAUS COPERNICUS: Yes. They did not like it when I said: To know that we know what we know, and to know that we do not know what we do not know, that is true knowledge.

JOHANNES KEPLER: Of course, well-stated.

NICOLAUS COPERNICUS: The universe has been wrought for us by a supremely good and orderly creator.

JOHANN KEPLER: Remember, that was back when I had that epiphany concerning "Platonic Solids" inscribed and circumscribed by spherical orbs?

NICOLAUS COPERNICUS: I do.

JOHANNES KEPLER: It all leads to the discovery of elliptical orbits we have already seen.

Columbus sees them both talk and turns to his friend Vasco da Gama.

CHRISTOPHER COLUMBUS: What are those two star-gazers talking about?

VASCO DA GAMA: No clue, but we do need to know what is going on up there *(pointing to the sky)* when we get in the middle of the sea.

CHRISTOPHER COLUMBUS: Of course! We shall prevail over all obstacles and distractions to unfailingly arrive…

Columbus stops in mid-sentence, hearing the wild sounds of a harpsichord keyboard.

VASCO DA GAMA: It is my old friend Dominico hammering away over there.

CHRISTOPHER COLUMBUS: Scarlatti!? The same who exploded with all those harpsichord sonatas when he got hooked up with the court in Spain?

VASCO DA GAMA: Yes! No other!

They both head over to where Scarlatti is still devouring the keyboards. Scarlatti abruptly stops playing and wheels around to da Gama.

DOMINICO SCARLATTI: Thought you would be chasing seagulls around the cape by now.

VASCO DA GAMA: Getting ready!

DOMINICO SCARLATTI: I always appreciated that you were more human than critical.

VASCO DA GAMA: That's what gives me the most pleasure in life.

DOMINICO SCARLATTI: Listen to this!

Scarlatti turns back to the harpsichord and plays more wild crescendos and almost off-key chords that get not-so-quickly resolved.

CHRISTOPHER COLUMBUS: We understand the power of music to inspire our adventures and world journeys.

Ferdinand Magellan, who has been circling around the yard for that last hour or so, comes forward to the group of explorers.

FERDINAND MAGELLAN: As a globe circumnavigator, I am also able to navigate my way through certain musical scores, especially Spanish, and of course I am a big Scarlatti fan. Who is your favorite?

CHRISTOPHER COLUMBUS: Without a doubt, Bach!

VASCO DA GAMA: Son?

CHRISTOPHER COLUMBUS: No, father...the father of all music.

One of Bach's cello suites begins as we see the entrance of Marco Polo, just back from all of his lengthy travels. Marco Polo is holding some nuts he brought as he glances over at the infamous group of worldly explorers.

MARCO POLO: One of these nuts is a meal for a man: both meat and drink.

J. S. Bach is now seen with his cello, playing his own suite as Scarlatti looks on approvingly.

JOHANN SEBASTIAN BACH: It is a pity we never crossed paths. Guess I just spent too much of my time in Leipzig.

DOMINICO SCARLATTI: Once I found the score for one of your violin partitas, and I drew ideas from it for over a year!

Bach glances over at the peace pipe Black Elk has just handed to Dali. Bach is obviously recalling a smoking experience.

JOHANN SEBASTIAN BACH: On land, sea, or home abroad, I smoke my pipe and worship God.

MARCO POLO: I have heard that you are just crazy for coffee, no matter where it's from. I had my first cup in Nubia, given to me by a woman so beautiful I just lost my breath.

JOHANN SEBASTIAN BACH: Ah!...How sweet coffee tastes! Lovelier than a thousand kisses, far sweeter than muscatel wine. *(He turns to Scarlatti)* Let me take a twirl here.

Bach sits down at the harpsichord and quiets the entire courtyard, even that far-flung gang of demigods, who were either uninvited or just never made it inside Plato's class. Carl Philipp Emanuel Bach strides up to come closer to his father.

CARL PHILIPP EMMANUEL BACH: A musician cannot move others until he, too, is moved.

Rumi is now back and moves his whirling dervish movements closer to the harpsichord as Isadora also comes around.

RUMI: Let beauty of what you love be what you do. What you seek is seeking you!

JOHANN SEBASTIAN BACH: I play the notes as they are written, but it is God who makes the music.

Plato now stands next to Aristotle, two fathers of two schools of thought, one the teacher of the other.

PROFESSOR PLATO: I wonder why so many of them never even bothered to show up for class?

ARISTOTLE: The heart is the seat of thought and reason.

ARISTOPHANES: I see all heart out there!

FOOL: All?! *(He points to the gang.)* What about them?

Hitler and the rest of the gang are clearly not enjoying this entertainment as Hitler motions his head in the direction of Bach.

ADOLF HITLER: Even though they refer to him as "father," he is not part of my "Fatherland!" Where do they get those ideas anyway?

Bach did not hear Hitler's exact words, but speaks as though he had.

JOHANN SEBASTIAN BACH: It is easy to play any instrument: all you have to do is touch the right key at the right time and the instrument plays itself.

KARL MARX: Just a show-off, hardly music to inspire a class struggle!

Groucho hears his false brother speaking.

GROUCHO MARX: As you struggle for class, he plays with it.

Groucho hands Bach his cigar.

GROUCHO MARX: Here, take a puff. Goes well with that coffee you are downing while I am here just clowning.

Bach continues on playing and improvising, with the cigar now puffing in his mouth as he smokes the keyboard.

Leon Trotsky has now moved closer to Marx and Hitler.

LEON TROTSKY: We Russians see music differently. How could I attach that "tune" to a worker's song?

JOHANN SEBASTIAN BACH: I worked hard. Anyone who works as hard as I did can achieve the same results...for God's glorification and refreshing the Spirit.

Looking over at the music Bach is now playing, Julius Caesar rides up and dismounts off his Roman Legion horse.

JULIUS CAESAR: I came, I saw, I conquered. Those damn Germanic tribes were always a constant threat to the order of our outermost border.

Beethoven is back again hearing the music of Bach, with Isadora still at his side as she leads him closer to Bach's harpsichord. Beethoven runs his hand over the side of the instrument and puts his ear funnel to his ear facing the keyboard.

LUDWIG VON BEETHOVEN: This is pure "Ode to Joy," first composed before I was even a boy.

PROFESSOR PLATO: Artists! How do we deal with them?

FOOL: That is "foolish thinking." Why are you stealing from me?

WILLIAM SHAKESPEARE: Stealing?! How do you think "I" wrote my tragedies and comedies—all taken from other stories.

ARISTOTLE: You know Plato, they are not even following my rules of storytelling.

FOOL: Don't think for a moment they ever read your "Poetics." You can still have class without clearly knowing the classics!

PROFESSOR PLATO: How did they get it?

Before Aristotle could explain, Shakespeare spots Julius Caesar in the middle of the yard near his horse.

WILLIAM SHAKESPEARE: How did he get here? I clearly don't remember writing this scene!

FOOL: You most likely didn't. Rumor has it that Bacon wrote everything.

WILLIAM SHAKESPEARE: Now I remember why I created you—for comic relief! You mean Francis Bacon, that snob! He didn't even bother to show up here, and I know he was invited by Plato.

FOOL: Look, there he is, over there talking to that other William— Blake!

WILLIAM SHAKESPEARE: William who?

FOOL: Never mind. I forgot you didn't possess a library when you were growing up. But it sure didn't slow you down from "writing" all those "history plays."

Francis Bacon is standing over there talking to William Blake

FRANCIS BACON: Did you know I wrote most of what is credited to Shakespeare?

WILLIAM BLAKE: Fascinating!

FRANCIS BACON: Though I have never seen your work, you are telling me that "visions" have come to you since you were a child?

WILLIAM BLAKE: Yes, I did many paintings to illustrate Dante's comedy, but never got to our own Shakespeare.

Bacon looks over at Plato and Aristotle near the classroom door and points to Plato.

FRANCIS BACON: We should return to his class.

WILLIAM BLAKE: What and miss this show! Here is where all the action is! There is no road back, only finding a way forward...

Satan reappears with his inner lining of crimson velvet as brilliant as ever.

SATAN: I demand to see Jesus. Where has that coward disappeared to?

FRANCIS BACON: You probably do not know how I view books, do you?

WILLIAM BLAKE: Illuminated books?

FRANCIS BACON: Yes, those too. Some are just to be tasted, others swallowed, some few to be slowly chewed and digested.

WILLIAM BLAKE: I can live with that.

Bacon now looks over to Satan and points to him.

FRANCIS BACON: ...and others to be tasted and spit out!

WILLIAM BLAKE: I was unaware he had a book.

FRANCIS BACON: He keeps rewriting it with his own blood, but the words refuse to stick as they flow too thick.

Satan now proceeds to call out Jesus.

SATAN: "Prince of Light!" Your very own shadow is here for a visit.

The voice of Jesus is audible, but he is not visible.

JESUS: I am everywhere you cannot see!

Hearing the voice of Jesus, Bach pauses for a moment in his playing.

JOHANN SEBASTIAN BACH: I am without my morning coffee, but I feel I just woke up! Harmony is next to godliness.

Jesus now directs his voice over to where Bach is playing.

JESUS: Who plays in my name shall see the promise land open before their eyes.

Plato now seizes this opportunity.

PROFESSOR PLATO: I promise you to return here to pass into that land.

Aristotle leans over to Plato to comment in a whisper.

ARISTOTLE: Brilliant! They have all abandoned my structure and just go where their "horse" takes them.

FOOL: As if mounted by some spirit. Why not! It makes sense because it's nonsense.

SATAN: I need to change that music to make it mine. Why should God get all the great tunes leaving me with just fortunes?

FOOL: Justice is just not just.

So far, only a handful have gone back into Plato's classroom. Kierkegaard is standing against the outside wall and never entered in the first place. He gives a shout over the din of the yard where Hitler and the rest of the outsider gang are stationed.

SOREN KIERKEGAARD: The tyrant dies and his rule is over, the martyr dies and his rule begins.

PROFESSOR PLATO: Why wasn't he invited?

ARISTOTLE: Purely an oversight.

SOREN KIERKEGAARD: Prayer does not change God, but it changes him who prays.

Satan is pacing, clearly discontent. His cape is flowing in the gusts of the wind.

SATAN: This is my kingdom!

BLACK ELK: Not while I make peace with my pipe. It all belongs to us!

SAMUEL BECKET: I have my faults, but changing my tune is not one of them.

WILLIAM BLAKE: See what I mean, Francis? Get your quill inked up and start writing. Let's see if you are who you say you are!

PETER: This should be as good a spot as any to lay the cornerstone of the first church. My name, after all, means "stone" or "rock."

JESUS: *(Disembodied voice)* You have the keys to the kingdom.

ARISTOTLE: Did you give the keys to Peter? How can we lock the school?

PROFESSOR PLATO: We have the "open door policy." Think "threshold," not door.

PETER: Whatever you bind on earth shall be bound in heaven. Whatever you lose on earth shall be lost in heaven.

FOOL: Here we go again with that "as above, so below" stuff.

PROFESSOR PLATO: A while ago there were so many of us—where did they all go?

ARISTOTLE: They must be free to come and go as they please.

PROFESSOR PLATO: As head of the Academy, I am here to guide them back.

ARISTOTLE: What can you offer that they cannot get on their own?

PROFESSOR PLATO: Dance of guidance!

FOOL: You serious? Anyone can dance anywhere they please.

PROFESSOR PLATO: Not that dance!

ARISTOTLE: Then what?

ARISTOPHANES: I am dying to know too!

Rumi and Isadora are whirling together like two binary stars as Kepler starts to notice their planetary style of dancing.

JOHANNES KEPLER: There is my "ellipsis!" Each dancer is a "point of focus."

NICOLAUS COPERNICUS: Where is my "sun" in the center?

JESUS: *(Disembodied voice)* I am here!

MARY: And I near!

PROFESSOR PLATO: By the way, what ever happened to our beloved "Lost Generation?"

ARISTOTLE: Who?

PROFESSOR PLATO: You know, that crowd of Hemingway, Fitzgerald, Picasso, etc.

ARISTOPHANES: They can easily find us, unless they are truly lost.

FRANCIS BACON: Truth is hard to tell; it sometimes needs fiction to make it plausible.

FOOL: You keep repeating yourself Sir Francis

WILLIAM BLAKE: Nothing so strange about that. Imagination IS Truth!

Another member of Plato's original list of invited students is now arriving quite late, but when we see who it is, there is no surprise there. It is Lewis Carroll, who coined "late for a very important date." But when Plato checks, it appears that Lewis Carroll is not on his list.

LEWIS CARROLL: If you do not know where you are going, any road will get you there.

FOOL: How about coming to work for me?

Aldous Huxley, roaming around the yard, passes by the classroom door, but shows no interest in entering. Aristophanes sees him and makes a comment to him.

ARISTOPHANES: I remember you. Doors of...

ALDOUS HUXLEY: ...Perception.

Aristophanes now points to the open door to Plato's Academy. Huxley notices and points to his own head.

ALDOUS HUXLEY: These doors, the ones that William Blake cleansed, remember?

Aristophanes glances over to Plato.

ARISTOPHANES: Let him go on his way.

Huxley continues walking and speaking out to no one in particular.

ALDOUS HUXLEY: Happiness is a hard master, particularly other people's happiness.

PROFESSOR PLATO: We didn't even get to cover that. I was saving it for now when they all return.

FOOL: You wish!

LEWIS CARROLL: Contrary to popular opinion, I am not, nor was I ever, a druggy. Occasionally I would enjoy a glass of sherry, or once in a while indulge in the opiate-infused drug laudanum, which was readily available to anyone who so desired. I never took any mind-altering drugs.

Aristophanes and Plato have already moved past Carroll and are trying to find that "Lost Generation."

ARISTOPHANES: Look! There is Hemingway!

Aristophanes motions to him. He is dressed like a bull fighter, maybe in a dramatic attempt to finally express his true inner being.

ERNEST HEMINGWAY: Happiness in intelligent people is the rarest thing I know.

PROFESSOR PLATO: We will cover that next, if you could come and join us, "Papa."

ERNEST HEMINGWAY: Wow! Even you know that!

Plato gestures over to Picasso.

PROFESSOR PLATO: I first heard your nickname from Picasso. Now, you look a bit unsure of yourself, which I never thought I would see in you.

ERNEST HEMINGWAY: Hesitation increases in relation to risk in equal proportion to age.

Fitzgerald now catches up and is walking a pace behind the two talking.

F. SCOTT FITZGERALD: That's a mouthful but hits me square...show me a hero and I'll write you a tragedy.

The Fool looks over at Hemingway and nods to him.

F. SCOTT FITZGERALD : Great art is the contempt of a great man for small art.

Henry Miller is till cruising around on his bicycle and now catches up to the "Lost Generation" group.

HENRY MILLER: I have no money, no resources, no hopes. I am the happiest man alive.

FOOL: Impressive! Go on Mr. Miller.

HENRY MILLER: The world dies over and over again, but the skeleton always gets up and walks.

PROFESSOR PLATO: How could I have left out this philosopher-cyclist?

HENRY MILLER: Imagination is the voice of daring. If there is anything Godlike about God it is that. He dared to imagine everything!

God, himself makes an unexpected appearance.

GOD: *(Disembodied voice, deeper than Jesus's)* Finally someone got it right!

ARISTOPHANES: You had given Miller up for lost, along with all those others who expatriated to Paris

PROFESSOR PLATO: A grave oversight.

F. SCOTT FITZGERALD: You know Ernest, you always had that ability to put down on paper what was on your mind. That is pure genius.

ERNEST HEMINGWAY: Got me the Nobel Prize, then in the end that "Nobel" GOT ME as "its" prize.

F. SCOTT FITZGERALD: I know you were never the same after that.

ERNEST HEMINGWAY: I love sleep. My life tends to fall apart when I am awake, you know?

Picasso is still there near them, listening.

PABLO PICASSO: It takes a long time to become young.

ERNEST HEMINGWAY: Don't think I'll make it.

PABLO PICASSO: It's all in the way you look at it.

ERNEST HEMINGWAY: How so?

PABLO PICASSO: The artist is a receptacle of emotions that come from all over the place: from a scrap of paper to a spider's web.

Rumi now whirls by, still together with Isadora in their "star dance."

RUMI: Beauty surrounds us, but usually we need to be walking in a garden to know it.

PROFESSOR PLATO: Who do we have so far who has come back in?

FOOL: Any votes for Hitler, Stalin or Caligula?

Plato glances over at the gang members, after hearing some of their names called out by the Fool. Hitler still appears to be angry at Bach and his harpsichord playing, and is seen mumbling something or other under his breath, making angry gestures in the direction of all that beauty of dance and music. Now he turns again to Karl Marx.

ADOLF HITLER: Did he just once happen to mention Siegfried and our rich Germanic folklore? He is German for God's sake.

Marx has a blank look on his face with apparently nothing to comment on.

ADOLF HITLER: Always citing God this and God that. Where is my beloved Wagner when I need him? The only one of the lot we can incorporate into our vision of the pure race.

As twilight approaches we start to hear first very softly, then louder, Wagnerian tone chords as he, himself, reappears wearing his usual artist's bonnet and velvet cape. His back is to the setting sun.

RICHARD WAGNER: I am convinced that there are universal currents of Divine Thought vibrating the "ether" everywhere, and that anyone who can feel these vibrations gets inspired.

ADOLF HITLER: That's my man!

PROFESSOR PLATO: He just has too much homework to do to catch up!

ARISTOTLE: And I won't always be here to bail him out.

PETER: He does not see the angles of the star.

Jesus is back in person with us.

JESUS: No one does. You need to *be* light to understand its angle!

MARY: I am to be that Muse that will inspire you and your followers.

PETER: My followers? Why?

PROFESSOR PLATO: Who, if any of them out there will be resurrected? Have their souls been saved?

Hildegard von Bingem is now singing a tune at the very threshold of the classroom as Plato looks on in admiration.

PROFESSOR PLATO: Welcome Hilde—you're in! Both you and Kierkegaard are the first to come through.

HILDEGARD VON BINGEM: William Blake and I draw "visions" from that same cloud-of-all-knowing.

PROFESSOR PLATO: Both of you have many talents in many fields— what a harvest!

William Blake is still over near Black Elk, playing the flute together with him, a combination of the Baroque flute with the Native American flute.

HILDEGARD VON BINGEM: I am crazy about his watercolor paintings, so dynamically done to illustrate the fluidity of the universe.

PROFESSOR PLATO: We want both of you to pass through, right Aristotle?

HILDEGARD VON BINGEM: The mystery of God hugs you in its all-encompassing arms.

Hildegard enters the classroom as she passes Samuel Becket, seated and still waiting at the entrance.

SAMUEL BECKET: The class is waiting here.

FOOL: Pain feeds the brain.

Aristotle looks over at the Fool, a furtive glance that judges his remark as utterly meaningless.

FOOL: Don't think about it as you are thinking about it.

PROFESSOR PLATO: No artists, plus no "fools" in my Republic, I have finally decided.

ARISTOTLE: Let's get organized here, and see who we'll have back and ultimately "reborn."

Isadora approaches the classroom threshold still with Beethoven close by.

LUDWIG VON BEETHOVEN: My art saved me from sure death of the spirit.

PROFESSOR PLATO: We welcome you, Herr Beethoven, and we recognize you as holder of the heavenly key to music and all the sound arts.

LUDWIG VON BEETHOVEN: There are many keys to a single keyhole. It's an entire ring!

Beethoven is still flailing his arms, still "conducting."

MICHELANGELO: Hey there, Fool! I loved what you said about "pain feeding the brain."

LUDWIG VON BEETHOVEN: Your Sistine Chapel has been compared to my Ninth Symphony in its sheer size and scope.

JESUS: That's what we do: become reborn! I am King of all this reawakening!

SOCRATES: Why was I killed, because…

FOOL: I have no clue, but I die to each moment and awaken in a second not forsaken.

Plato now is motioning to Gurdjieff to please join them in the classroom. Gurdjieff still holds the shovel high above his head, then bring it down to come over and stand in the yard next to the sword and that large oversized paint brush.

G.I. GURDJIEFF: These are the tools of the trade, no matter what is actually done or made.

SOCRATES: They had to poison me for knowing nothing, especially for knowing I knew nothing, yet Plato was encouraged to live on knowing everything.

Through an act of special magic, Merlin has appeared out of a cloud of smoke in front of the classroom door right near where Becket was planted.

PROFESSOR PLATO: Look, Aristotle!

Plato has totally ignored the appearance of Merlin and is looking at a much more compelling picture. Moses is coming towards them, parting the two groups of students like the Red Sea.

PROFESSOR PLATO: Moses! My God! You can pass this class.

MOSES: I imagined no less.

ARISTOTLE: We are your Red Sea!

MOSES: I have been a stranger in a foreign land until now. Our journey together is just beginning.

Plato now eyes Einstein, who is looking at both groups of superstars gathered in the yard.

ALBERT EINSTEIN: Who can doubt that you, Moses, were and still are a better leader than the conniving Machiavelli?

MACHIAVELLI: Politics have no relation to morals. Never was anything achieved without danger.

MOSES: I well know how to detect and capture that gleam of light flashing across my mind with deep insight.

MACHIAVELLI: You became a true "Prince," not by birth, but because of your birth.

PROFESSOR PLATO: True, but "you" have done less to improve our condition through your calculating political shrewdness that in the long run breeds general distrust.

ARISTOPHANES: Then he will fail to pass through this hallway of learning?

FOOL: It's a cinch that this man is no prince.

ARISTOTLE: How many can we take back in to the Academy?

PROFESSOR PLATO: My background is from the group of Pythagoras after studying with Socrates.

FOOL: Don't be fooled, Aristotle, by his geometry in those "humming" of strings, or that "music" he discovers of how the spheres of the celestial world are placed.

Pythagoras is, of course, nearby on this one and is quick to respond.

PYTHAGORAS: Listen you fool! You say little in many words, yet cannot find a few to say a lot.

FOOL: I am not surprised.

PYTHAGORAS: You must know that the oldest and shortest of words, yes and no, require the most thought.

Plato is still thinking about numbers in his Academy.

PROFESSOR PLATO: The magic number is thirty-three!

HIPPOCRATES: The number of vertebrae in the spinal column…

JESUS: And the exact number of years I had to live, die and be resurrected.

PROFESSOR PLATO: You have passed!

JESUS: You have it all backwards, Plato. Those who have managed to "escape" this room, this tomb, have a chance.

PROFESSOR PLATO: Then they are all the resurrected and reborn?

JESUS: Inside each one.

PROFESSOR PLATO: What about those shadowy characters who never ever came to any of my classes?

Satan has been roving freely around the yard, and now is passing by the two conversing.

SATAN: We shall have our day in the sun! Or should I say moon?

FOOL: Just say nothing. You were better off.

Van Gogh had been in almost stoic meditation of the skies and stars for some time now.

VINCENT VAN GOGH: I believe my "Starry Night" painting is my ticket to "Paradise."

PROFESSOR PLATO: Let's let Master Dante be the judge of that.

WILLIAM SHAKESPEARE: Well, if you want to go that route, *Hamlet* is a "masterpiece in ambivalence," which would make it a strong candidate for something—who knows what—perhaps Purgatory?

FOOL: Francis Bacon, can you come to our aid here? We just cannot let this "be" or not "be."

ARISTOPHANES: If there are too many here to be resurrected that could present a problem, right, Señor Dante?

DANTE ALIGHIERI: My *Divine Comedy* is half divine and half comedy. It's its own remedy.

FOOL: Only the true, great artists do not age, because they are able to innovate and invent new forms, new colors, new structures and ultimately recreate themselves.

PROFESSOR PLATO: Wow! My fool! Who knew, but you do. I have just given you a passing grade. Come on through!

FOOL: Your school is not for a fool, though if wisely employed, could be a useful tool.

DANTE ALIGHIERI: I took you all to Hell and back, which should count for something more than a polished coin tossed into a wishing well.

PROFESSOR PLATO: You are a wealth of knowledge. You brought us back, and on through Purgatory, and then to Paradise.

ARISTOTLE: I am devoted to have you declared as person most voted.

PROFESSOR PLATO: There are way too many candidates to be chosen as official Academy members.

FOOL: Why so sure they even want it? I don't see too many of them doing their best to get through your schoolroom door.

Genghis Khan is still on his horse, and appears to be in command of his own situation as he bellows out his remark.

GENGHIS KHAN: My school is contained in my one thought of pure action!

Joan of Arc now rides up right alongside Genghis Kahn.

JOAN OF ARC: Never thought of us riding together but here we are.

FOOL: My thoughts continue to be wild and crazy of late. All of life and history, past, future and present will unfold before us to behold.

PROFESSOR PLATO: None can say in all truth who among us can be saved, and who is without salvation and utterly depraved.

After being away for a while, assumed to have been poisoned and killed, Socrates resurfaces.

SOCRATES: I am still without true knowledge, yet that in itself I know to be true.

PROFESSOR PLATO: My very first mentor and initial pillar of our triad. Your method of question and answer has been cemented into our classical tradition.

SOCRATES: My Spirit is the world, and its words to describe it are richer and more ambiguous than science alone could ever grasp.

ARISTOTLE: What do you mean by science?

SOCRATES: What is known, or what you can split or cleave before you take your leave.

PROFESSOR PLATO: I have heard that you must not talk before you know.

SOCRATES: Then I shall remain silent, and now have an even better reason to do so.

Musical chords now come from the Isolde and Tristan opera overture as Richard Wagner strides towards Plato still wearing his customary beret and silken gown.

RICHARD WAGNER: Imagination creates reality.

PROFESSOR PLATO: That simple?

RICHARD WAGNER: Yes, and all of my music I score use horns as the foundation ore.

Sandro Botticelli has arrived, though also not on Plato's original invitation list, he has nevertheless made his way from Italy to the school.

SANDRO BOTTICELLI: As a Florentine, I came became of Leonardo and Michelangelo.

Karl Marx is still pacing and obviously deep in thought over his own ideas, still carrying around that large manuscript of "Das Kapital." Marx is completely unaware of Botticelli's linear sense of form, strong resonant color schemes and graceful costuming that is said to epitomize the spirit of the Renaissance.

KARL MARX: Who has nowadays, and especially in the "class struggle," any use for your contours and outlines you depict in your nudes?

Groucho Marx has been marauding around and now shoots out a remark.

GROUCHO MARX: You question women?

SANDRO BOTTICELLI: I follow the line of beauty, not of questioning!

PROFESSOR PLATO: Artist or not, you are in, Sandro!

They are interrupted by Jesus over in another corner of the yard, with his tomb and stone situation.

JESUS: Who wants to help me roll away this massive stone blocking the very way for all of us to atone?

GAUTAMA BUDDHA: Count me in!

The two alone manage to roll it away at last.

RICHARD WAGNER: I am convinced that there are interesting invisible currents of Divine thought vibrating in the "ether" everywhere that can easily explain the source of inspiration.

JESUS: He got it, Plato!

FOOL: But who can get through your entire Ring Cycle?

RICHARD WAGNER: It is not for fools!

JESUS: Who else?

Igor Stravinsky has been wandering all around with Nijinsky and the other Russians, as well as trying to get a connection with Bach, though unsuccessfully.

IGOR STRAVINSKY: Me!

PROFESSOR PLATO: Who are you? I don't remember you, nor recognize your voice.

IGOR STRAVINSKY: Igor!

From across the yard, Lenin intervenes with answer.

VLADIMIR LENIN: One of us!

IGOR STRAVINSKY: I am an inventor of music.

FOOL: *(Under his breath)* Oh, so that's what you call it!

Mozart is literally now doing cartwheels around the yard.

WOLFGANG AMADEUS MOZART: Harmony IS God!

JESUS: Amen!

PROFESSOR PLATO: Hey, everybody just settle down here, or we'll never get through this.

CHRISTOPHER COLUMBUS: Just give up your quest. Let us in our own way discover this New World for you

ARISTOTLE: He is right, Plato. Look at all your former students, and those new ones, and that whole gang over there you refused admission to.

FOOL: Who are we to judge, anyway? This is not all a test, nor is it just jest.

We now hear some strange sounding viols coming from all sides of the yard.

DANTE ALIGHIERI: I wrote somewhere about this kind of music at one point coming to us from Paradise.

Nefertiti turns away from Leonardo and his painting for a moment.

NEFERTITI: Sounds eerily Egyptian, like they are all playing low sound flutes on the banks of the Nile.

LEONARD DAVINCI: It reaches way beyond the tips of my "brush imagination."

ALBERT EINSTEIN: It is the "strings of the universe" vibrating in unison, tying space and time together. That is exactly why I studied the violin.

PROFESSOR PLATO: Striking this musical chord where it "hurts" is our renowned "Father," the illustrious Johann Sebastian Bach!

FOOL: He is already in the classroom studying for his next composition. Over one thousand already, not counting the multitude now lost forever by careless copyists.

Bach hears his name and comes out to where they are.

JOHANN SEBASTIAN BACH: I would have no problem living in "Paradise" as long as there can be fresh coffee available for all composers and performers.

DANTE ALIGHIERI: Don"t worry. We have taken care of that. Can't remember who tipped us off, but it's all set up.

JOHANN SEBASTIAN BACH: I'm in! Let's do it!

DANTE ALIGHIERI: I have a spot for you with Mary, the Celestial Rose, in the tenth heaven where in a flash of light you can become one with God!

JOHANN SEBASTIAN BACH: My organ playing and composing describe all the details of this Celestial Rose.

DANTE ALIGHIERI: It is Beatrice who has successfully guided me on this journey through Heaven.

JOHANNES KEPLER: I am able to crunch the numbers to calculate all of the details for this complete journey.

CARL JUNG: We are living now at the right time for what you, Greeks, called a "metamorphosis of the gods."

ARISTOTLE: Do you know about this, Plato?

CARL JUNG: We are all symbols of our own transformation!

FOOL: As the "fool," I can see my own reflections in a pool.

SOCRATES: I have no secrets. I am open to the world!

FOOL: Is that why they had you finally poisoned?

SOCRATES: Still wondering that.

PROFESSOR PLATO: As my teacher, you taught me not to make that mistake.

ARISTOPHANES: I heard somewhere that certain defeats are more triumphant than victories.

Moliere now comes to stand firmly by the side of Aristophanes.

MOLIERE: My duty as a comedian is to correct men by amusing them.

Sir Francis drake has now arrived to help all in guiding this journey home.

SIR FRANCIS DRAKE: Sic Parvis Magra.

FOOL: You are kidding, right, Sir? Latin now?

SIR FRANCIS DRAKE: My Queen taught me during my stay at her court.

PROFESSOR PLATO: You must know that, fool: Great things come from small things.

FOOL: I only knew that I was great.

PROFESSOR PLATO: Circumnavigating the globe, Mr. Drake, you must have concluded life is circular—basic geometry.

Drake makes no comment, but is content to drink it all in like a greedy pirate of the senses.

SOCRATES: You have an acute sense of observation. I trained you well!

Kierkegaard, who was already back in the classroom, speaks up.

SOREN KIERKEGAARD: If I ever return to my homeland, wherever that is, I will do it with a gait as steady as a postman's.

GAUTAMA BUDDHA: You have heard me advise to "walk on," that's the "talk" that takes off.

SOREN KIERKEGAARD: I am who I am. That, I have faced, which is what changes what I am.

FOOL: I don't ever remember seeing you in the school.

SOCRATES: Where does happiness lie—inside or outside?

Mozart has quietly returned to the class, one of Plato's favorite because his music is composed in the "classical style."

FOOL: He is "pure class"; does he still need yours?

Hildegard von Bingam is now by Mozart's side

HILDEGARD VON BINGEM: You might say, Wolfgang, that happiness is where melody meets harmony.

WOLFGANG AMADEUS MOZART: I call that God!

Since Plato has extended the invitation for all to come and attend his class, Goliath, of all people came.

GOLIATH: I am God!

Both Mozart and Hildegard ignore this massive intrusion. Moliere is simply admiring this whole unbelievable scene.

MOLIERE: What a baseline!

King David now puts down the lyre and puts a flute to his lips to blow.

KING DAVID: With all the time I spent in the battlefield, I am now more than ready for this field of music.

FOOL: How delightful! *(He looks at Plato.)* And you Professor?

PROFESSOR PLATO: We must reacquaint the mind with all those realities during one's previous existence of the soul.

ARISTOTLE: What do you say to that, Socrates?

SOCRATES: Our only escape is to acknowledge that we already know what we need to know.

ARISTOTLE: I understand, Plato, why you point your finger upward, nevertheless I will point mine outward from myself.

FOOL: *(Laughing)* You really believe that the natural forces can be explained by logic and reason?

ARISTOTLE: Ultimately, the Planet Earth is round...

FOOL: We're going round and round here with this.

Henry Miller comes around again, speaking of around. And yells out at Aristotle:

HENRY MILLER: Are you happy?...I am a happy rock!

FOOL: That's heavy!

ARISTOTLE: It is a fine balance of mental and physical well-being.

FOOL: That is one fine answer.

The gang outside the school room hears through the grapevine that class is back in session for their final test. Stalin looks over at Hitler.

JOSEPH STALIN: Should we terrorize them like the allies did to us? We lost more than all the other countries combined.

ADOLF HITLER: No, I have another idea. Now, this is *our* "camp of concentration."

KARL MARX: They are in "there" struggling to have class.

GROUCHO MARX: Here we go with your old class struggle again.

KARL MARX: Your "bourgeois humor" belongs in there.

Marx quickly points to Plato's classroom. Dali is still high on Navajo Medicine with the generous help of Black Elk's peace pipe and is engaging in a kind of surreal dance.

IGOR STRAVINSKY: Where is "my" Nijinsky? I need him now!

FOOL: You are mad, Mr. Marx, because your proletarian revolution has failed to take place all over the world.

JOSEPH STALIN: We seemed to have made out just fine here in our New Union!

KARL MARX: We need to doubt everything!

FOOL: Even the rising sun!

ADOLF HITLER: Get that Fool out of here!

Hitler lifts up a large club-like weapon with a swastika carving on the side of it.

FOOL: I am on my way back to school, and can hear Plato calling my name now!

Goliath sticks his giant head out of the school room window and yells out.

GOLIATH: Plato, the headmaster, has declared all are welcome in here. That's how I got in!

Genghis Kahn is still swooping around on his horse.

GENGHIS KHAN: I can because I "Kahn"!

FOOL: And we "would" if we "could."

Bach is back! He is inside the classroom along with Michelangelo, with his tools all spread out ready to sculpt his next masterpiece. He eyes the gargantuan Goliath.

MICHELANGELO: I am in the mood to sculpt the "naked truth"!

FOOL: For you, the "Emperor" is always wearing no clothes. Literally *and* figuratively.

MICHELANGELO: How did you "figure" that out?

FOOL: Clothes both reveal and hide. The truth is always naked— even when clothed.

MICHELANGELO: What's that?

FOOL: Diaphanous! You see through!

LEONARD DA VINCI: You are wasting words with him, you fool. What his sculpture reveals is there has been a battle here in Florence. We are fierce competitors, yes it's true. It's been a battle for class, not a class struggle.

PROFESSOR PLATO: That's what I have been saying! Now is the time for everyone's final test!

HENRY MILLER: I put down everything of mine in those three volumes called "The Rosy Crucifixion"!

JESUS: I have returned after mine!

Now everyone is everywhere, the gang and students commingling.

SATAN: Much to my chagrin. But the battle rages on. Trust me, I will respond later through the Arts!

NOSTRADAMUS: As a physician by trade, I can tell you that things are not well in the arts that are being made, yet I have done my part in treating the Black Death by removing many infected corpses.

PROFESSOR PLATO: Where can we find all this?

NOSTRADAMUS: It has been recorded in my book, "The Centuries," that refers to the number of verses in each section.

WILLIAM BLAKE: What is your system for "seeing" your "visions?"

NOSTRADAMUS: I simply stare into water or a burning flame late at night.

WILLIAM BLAKE: I simply do nothing, and an entire painting will flash before my eyes.

The biblical Job has come on the scene here near the end.

JOB: Is that how you painted and illustrated my plight?

WILLIAM BLAKE: In a whirlwind of inspiration.

JOB: I felt the brush flow in your mind that brought me forth in a glow.

WILLIAM BLAKE: You know well my show!

JOB: A small speck of me is in all of you, whether still bound or set free.

ARISTOPHANES: Is it still there after this civilizing effect has turned me from princely to frog-like?

Hieronymus Bosch now makes his very first appearance at the school in a very timely fashion. Plato had completely overlooked him when he sent out the invitations.

HIERONYMUS BOSCH: My depiction of Job was entirely different from yours, Mr. Blake, though I pose the question: what is the potential man, after all?

FOOL: Pray, do tell us!

HIERONYMUS BOSCH: Is he not the sum of all that is human— including the "Divine?"

Churchill arrives in the class and responds on cue.

WINSTON CHURCHILL: Human beings are of three classes: those who are toiled to death, those who are worried to death, and those who are bored to death.

Darwin is still pacing around outside the classroom undecided if he enters or not.

CHARLES DARWIN: Plato's class bored me, that's why I can't return.

FOOL: That would take an evolutionary leap!

SOREN KIERKEGAARD: Or leap of faith!

ALBERT EINSTEIN: Or quantum leap!

G.I. GURDJIEFF: To reap is to leap after we have declared our "war on sleep."

Outside and pacing back and forth there is more grumbling coming from that band of outsiders who never entered Plato's classroom as if no one is even close to being happy about anything.

JOSEPH STALIN: We all live through the nightmare we created.

Gurdjieff has gone outside still wearing his Russian fur hat, bottle of vodka in his hand.

G.I. GURDJIEFF: Take a drink, Joe. To your nation of sheep, all still very much asleep!

JOSEPH STALIN: Only your name sounds Russian. Drinking "our" vodka shows immense disrespect!

Gurdjieff is still seen with the bottle of vodka in one hand and still brandishing the shovel in the other. Stravinsky has finally located Nijinsky who is dancing with Isadora to a Scriabin Sonata.

IGOR STRAVINSKY: That's not what I trained you for! What about dancing to *my* music?

VASLAV NIJINSKY: "It" danced through me, yet did not stay to see another day.

IGOR STRAVINSKY: All around me I see the corruption of monotone imaginations!

Isadora and Nijinsky continue their Scriabin dance, ignoring Igor. Now Leonardo chimes in.

LEONARD DA VINCI: You can only free yourself through discipline!

G.I. GURDJIEFF: Always avoid involuntary action. If you don't have a critical mind, your journey here had been a wasted time.

HENRY MILLER: No one sets about saving the world unless he has first experienced the miracle of personal salvation.

FOOL: Enter Shakespeare! Now, we can use your words.

FRANCIS BACON: Did you call me fool?

FOOL: Not really, but better than I expected: the real deal!

FRANCIS BACON: Imagination was given to man to compensate for what he is not; a sense of humor to console him for what he is.

Van Gogh is still struggling with both his art and most heroically with himself.

VINCENT VAN GOGH: I simply hope I shall one day be able to make some drawings in which there is something human.

DANTE ALIGHIERI: O human race, born to fly upward, wherefore at a little wind dost thou so fall!

ARISTOTLE: You keeping track of all this?

PROFESSOR PLATO: Trying to evaluate, but we are missing so many who are still out there mingling around.

ARISTOTLE: It is your Academy!

PROFESSOR PLATO: We are so far from the solidity of an ideal form.

We shift our attention back outside to catch up on their goings on. Darwin is still parading back and forth near the threshold of the classroom door.

CHARLES DARWIN: You must, however, acknowledge, as it seems to me that man with all his noble qualities, still bears in his bodily frame the indelible stamp of his lowly origin.

ARISTOPHANES: According to Dante, we have three worlds which are all self-contained: Inferno, Purgatorio and Paradiso.

HENRY MILLER: Certainly, the Paradise, whatever, wherever it be, contains flaws, paradisal flaws if you will. If it did not, you would be incapable of drawing the hearts of men and angels.

ARISTOTLE: Our work should eschew subjectivity in order to illumine in form the things that change or do not change in the life of a man.

PROFESSOR PLATO: Back to my Ideal Forms!

DANTE ALIGHIERI: We were not made to live as brutes, but to follow virtue and knowledge in search of that ideal form.

HIERONYMUS BOSCH: Feast your eyes on my "Garden of Delights!" I set out to paint "paradise" but in the end hovered between "purgatory" and "inferno."

JESUS: We are still "cleansing our doors."

GAUTAMA BUDDHA: To cross their "thresholds."

SALVADOR DALI: I am the "door!"

ERIK SATIE: Since I was the very first to enter Plato's Academy, I would like to be one of the last to speak.

PROFESSOR PLATO: By all means.

ERIK SATIE: Before I compose any piece of music, I walk around it several times, accompanied by myself.

FOOL: And I pictured myself alone!

ERIK SATIE: I have taken the liberty to call my old friend Jean Cocteau for our class finals.

Jean Cocteau has already arrived and been with Satie for a while.

JEAN COCTEAU: Mirrors should think long before they reflect. Art is a marriage of the conscious and the unconscious.

CARL JUNG: I wish I had said that, talk about stealing your thunder.

JEAN COCTEAU: You still have your "lightning": the symbol!

CARL JUNG: Let's have a really good wine tonight and just enjoy the sunset.

GAUTAMA BUDDHA: And a slice of chocolate cake.

FOOL: But what of the Mind, my great masters?

JESUS: It is no other than mountains, rivers and the wide earth, the sun, the moon and the stars.

MARY: I dance in that Robe of Stars!

Outside again, we see a wandering Dostoyevsky, together with Stravinsky and Nijinsky.

FYODOR DOSTOYEVSKY: The cleverest of all is the one who calls himself a fool at least once a month.

FOOL: You can all be me, it is so easy. Anyone can do it.

PROFESSOR PLATO: This final class has become a farce. Where are the tests? Who passes, who fails?

ARISTOTLE: As your most famous student, I cannot answer that.

PROFESSOR PLATO: Who will come forward now to have the final word: the women warriors, the musicians, the philosophers, the conquerors, the mystics, or the misfits?

FOOL: I vote for the misfits, Master Instructor!

ARISTOPHANES: You are not even part of this circus, now are you?

FOOL: I accept the role as the clown.

VASLAV NIJINSKY: People like and don't like eccentricities. Therefore they will leave me alone, saying that I am a "mad clown." I guess there are two of us now.

FOOL: You can have the role. You dance better.

FRIEDRICH NIETZSCHE: I have heard enough and had enough. The higher we soar, the smaller we appear to those who can't fly.

RUMI: This is our quest: the flight of light!

GAUTAMA BUDDHA: Enjoy!

FRIEDRICH NIETZSCHE: Live! This is not a dress rehearsal.

WILLIAM SHAKESPEARE: Even though it's all a stage.

RENE DESCARTES: Except our own thoughts, there is nothing absolutely in our power.

Black Elk has been inching his way towards the classroom and now is at the doorway.

BLACK ELK: It does not require many words to speak the Truth.

Nefertiti is now happy as Leonardo shows his finished portrait of her for all to see.

NEFERTITI: As Ruler of the Nile, it is the longest river running though us all.

Without much ado, Madame Blavatsky has entered the classroom for the very first time. She finds Moses easily, who has once more parted the way for her entrance.

MADAME BLAVATSKY: The Universe is worked and guided from within outwards.

FOOL: Could we add "As within, so without" to our age-old standard, "As above, so below"?

PROFESSOR PLATO: I think you have now nailed it my dear Fool.

FOOL: The clown has spoken! What does it matter.

MADAME BLAVATSKY: Matter? It matters! Matter is Spirit at its lowest level, whereas Spirit is Matter at its highest level.

IGOR STRAVINSKY: When I compose I try to make some sense out of this world, this state of class. My art opposes it, by organizing it.

Franz Liszt was invited by Plato, but has just shown up at the last minute here. Robert Schumann came with Liszt.

FRANZ LISZT: My approach, Igor, has been much more romantic and dramatic. At times I feel as if I am just hurling my javelin into the future's infinite space.

ROBERT SCHUMANN: I just play as if always within earshot of a master. Don't worry who is listening, if anyone. Just be that creative genius you have worked so hard all your life to become.

SATAN: I will have the final word!

MADAME BLAVATSKY: It has been proven that you "are" that fiery Red Dragon of Lucifer, who bears the Light. You are in us. You are our Mind!

SATAN: I am your trainer. THE trainer on Earth!...My Kingdom!

JESUS: You are right, mine is another!

MADAME BLAVATSKY: One of you "on" my mind and the other "out" of my mind.

FOOL: I choose "mindless." Thinking always got me into trouble.

LUDWIG VON BEETHOVEN: Emotion is the key word here. Feelings in movement. When I see you dance, Isadora, it's pure emotion!

ISADORA DUNCAN: I am merely the "face" of the ancient Greek vase, turning round and round like the wheel of the "thrown" clay vessel.

MICHELANGELO: You are a whirling sculpture. Your emotions are the chisel.

PABLO PICASSO: We are all "sculptures" of our own making, no matter who we are or what is our undertaking.

JOHANN SEBASTIAN BACH: How can we balance improvisation with our overall schematic design?

WOLFGANG AMADEUS MOZART: You do it in your grand Fugue, to provoke in the rest of us grand intrigue"

From outside, a surprisingly similar dialog is taking place, though neither group can hear the other.

JOSEPH STALIN: When your head becomes a hammer, it is easier to nail it.

ADOLF HITLER: I once heard one of my marshals telling me that, overcome by anger, he is possessed with an unmanageable desire to shove his hand down his tormenter's throat and try to pull out the heart.

ALEXANDER THE GREAT: My teacher, Aristotle, always reminded me that "character is fate," quoting Heraclitus.

FOOL: When you are damned, you are doomed.

SAMUEL BECKET: It is all gloom and doom.

FRANZ KAFKA: This IS my trial...to stop being a beetle.

PROFESSOR PLATO: Just for all here to know, no diplomas will be issued.

ARISTOTLE: But it does not mean all have passed.

Satan suddenly barges into the classroom.

SATAN: My planet earth is a school that I reign over. What you have staged here is a sham that proves nothing.

JESUS: Don't tempt me again. I have been through your "school," been found guilty of "not doing wrong," and punished. I arose from your "dead state" to my former "future state."

PETER: That rock you pushed away to arise became my cornerstone upon which we have set our "base tone."

PYTHAGORAS: God built the universe on numbers then fell silent. A fool is known by his speech.

FOOL: How else! I am paid by the line.

Abraham Lincoln has walked all the way through the snow to get to the school he wanted to get to know.

ABRAHAM LINCOLN: We are not worried, Professor Plato, if we are not worthy of being recognized, yet we still strive to be worthy of it.

ARISTOPHANES: Your harmonica playing has done you well.

ABRAHAM LINCOLN: I can only speak when my mind is empty. It creates a kind of vacuum that quickly filled with ideas.

ARISTOTLE: Nature abhors a vacuum.

PROFESSOR PLATO: You are right. I have changed my mind!

He motions to the courtyard. Out there, Hemingway is still prancing around in his bullfighter's garb, together with Fitzgerald in his white dinner jacket.

F. SCOTT FITZGERALD: I am taken back to those very early days when it all seemed a dream, a kind of chemical madness.

FOOL: Which I obviously have never grown out of.

PROFESSOR PLATO: There should be no more waiting for graduation!

John Dowland is also strolling around the yard playing his lute and softly singing.

JOHN DOWLAND: Who loves not music and the heavenly muse, that man God ignores.

Now again the voice of God booms.

GOD: *(Disembodied voice)* I AM the Harmony of the Spheres!

SATAN: I am that dissonance that drives the dance.

JOHANN SEBASTIAN BACH: There you have it: the major and minor chords!

SATAN: Who said I was "minor"? I am a major success the world over.

WILLIAM SHAKESPEARE: This stage is as good as any!

Leonardo da Vinci goes to the center of this stage now.

LEONARD DA VINCI: Iron rusts from disuse; water loses its purity from stagnation...even more does inaction sap the vigor of the mind.

GEORGE BERNARD SHAW: The mind is a muscle.

BLACK ELK: Wherever you are is the center of the universe! We are as important as we are unimportant.

PROFESSOR PLATO: The most important part of your "circle of friends" is the "circle."

FOOL: Don't try to fool me with "King Arther's Round Table."

PROFESSOR PLATO: Yes, I need twelve to come forward with their "elixir" they've won.

Plato surveys the field again, looking out onto the yard, as well as inside, where each participant by now has his own registration card. Heraclitus now comes forward to announce his candidacy.

HERACLITUS: You cannot step into the same class twice.

FOOL: We all know that one well. Both we, as well as the class, have become very different.

HERACLITUS: Well done, Fool! Between all things lies a hidden connection.

FOOL: Even among this motley crowd gathered here?

HERACLITUS: Especially! Fire unites us all!

FOOL: Making it no longer a "burning question." *(Laughing)*

PROFESSOR PLATO: Congratulations! You are the very first to pass!

HERACLITUS: I should like to be remembered for my Cosmology.

Plato and Aristotle survey the room again, and the yard.

ERNEST HEMINGWAY: Now I deeply regret having shot myself. I was at the end of my rope, no hope of writing as I had, nothing really to live for.

Plato is obviously moved now by Hemingway, even the Fool now is quiet.

ERNEST HEMINGWAY: Death resolved nothing, and even added more pain, now that there are no more possibilities—just the deepest regrets.

PROFESSOR PLATO: Just this realization now is your "elixir." You are the first of your "Lost Generation" to be now "found."

PABLO PICASSO: I do not seek. I find!

LEONARD DA VINCI: I know you have a deep connection with Raphael as you found out. For me, as I have already said, simplicity is the ultimate sophistication.

PROFESSOR PLATO: I can pass you on the strength of that phrase Mr. Da Vinci.

FOOL: But sophistication is simply not simple.

ARISTOPHANES: Dear Fool, you cannot always have the last word.

More music from the strolling John Dowland fills the yard and the minds of the listeners.

JOHN DOWLAND: I have cured insanity with my playful chords and turned a simple sound into a beguiling musical round.

Beethoven is now in a rare and sublime state as he whirls around and around in the yard, together with Isadora, just like binary stars. We hear powerful low voices singing "Ode to Joy."

~ Fin ~

About the Author and Artist

David L. Laing is a visionary selftaught artist and writer currently living and working in Seattle, Washington. His works in oil, acrylic, watercolor, and pen and ink drawing have been exhibited in South America, the United States, and Europe.

In his early twenties David trekked to South America with no money, in hopes of finding or founding a "New Paris for artists." Two months later and thirty pounds lighter, he limped into São Paulo, Brazil, having traversed the entire continent overland, nearly ten thousand miles, surviving purely on his own wits and with the aid of a few helpful souls. David spent over fifteen years in Brazil writing, drawing and painting, and composing music.

Since his return to the USA, David has focused on book publishing of his own novels, art books, and compilations of his articles. *Solar Codex: A Light Odyssey* and *Notes from the Milky Way* are the first two volumes in the seriess of Cosmic Adventure novels. At present, he is working on three other novels to complete the series and is preparing for publication many new books of drawings, articles, dialogs, plays, and screenplays. Nearly all of David's written work is lavishly illustrated with literally hundreds of drawings, all hand-inked by him.

Connect with David L. Laing

Purchase artwork

Illustrations in this book may be purchased at ArtPal. Many more drawings and paintings from David L. Laing's other books and themed collections are available at ArtPal.com/davidllaing as fine art prints, canvas prints, custom framed prints, and even on mugs.

Connect online

- **Website:** Find David's books, artwork and more at www.davidllaing.com.

- **Email newsletter:** Subscribe at davidllaing.com for news about book releases, art collections, exhibits, and more.

- **Instagram**: Follow David at instagram.com/davidl.laing/

- **Twitter:** Follow David at twitter.com/davidllaing9.

- **YouTube:** See book trailers and animated illustrations at tinyurl.com/cosmic-art-center-videos.

Artsana video

Watch the video of David's art book, *Artsana, 35 Sacred Yoga Asanas Expressed Through Art*, at tinyurl.com/artsana-video. Produced by One Field Media, www.onefieldmedia.com, and

David L. Laing, this short film features eight extraordinary yogis, accompanied with music by Andre Feriante, www.andreferiante.com.

Books by David L. Laing

Art and Coloring Books

Higher Glyphs

Artsana: 35 Sacred Yoga Asanas Expressed Through Art

Alpha 2 Zulu: Military Alphabet Coloring Book

AlphaBetter: Coloring Book of Letters and Numbers

Ancient Runes: For Coloring and Meditation

Willing Evolution

Dance of the Dance

Beyond the Box–Illustrated Articles

Beyond the Box, Volume 1

Beyond the Box, Volume 2

Beyond the Box, Volume 3 [Forthcoming]

Beyond the Box, Volume 4 [Forthcoming]

Becoming Human Series–Aphorisms

Not Yet Human

Almost Human

Just Human

Fully Human

Beyond Human [Forthcoming]

Cosmic Adventure Quartet—Novels

Solar Codex: A Light Odyssey

Notes from the Milky Way

Pentagram Rising [Forthcoming]

Prometheus Reforged [Forthcoming]

www.ingramcontent.com/pod-product-compliance
Lightning Source LLC
Chambersburg PA
CBHW060752050426
42449CB00008B/1372